SOCIAL REALITY

Perspectives and Understanding

Edited by

JANAK PANDEY

CONCEPT PUBLISHING COMPANY, NEW DELHI 110015

ISBN 81-7022-199-4

First published 1988

Published by

Naurang Rai
Concept Publishing Company
H-13 Bali Nagar
NEW DELHI - 110015 (India)

Printed at

Taj Press
A 35/4 Maya Puri
NEW DELHI

PREFACE

The project of this book was first conceived during an interdisciplinary seminar on "perspectives on perception and understanding of social reality" held in April 1983, at the Centre of Advanced Study in Psychology, University of Allahabad. The seminar participants were from various disciplines, such as, psychology, sociology, history, and literature. The present volume primarily constitutes revised form of some selected papers which were initially presented in the seminar. It also includes a paper on social reality and public policy by Dr. (Mrs.) S.Radhakrishnan and an introduction by the editor. We hope that this book will be particularly useful for the social scientists who face the growing challenges of scientific understanding of the social reality.

In preparation of this book, we received considerable support from the contributors and from the colleagues who participated in the seminar. Encouragement provided by Professor R.C. Tripathi and Professor R.K. Naidu to complete this book is highly appreciated. We are thankful to the University Grants Commission, New Delhi for providing support for the seminar and publication of this book.

Centre of Advanced Study in Psychology JANAK PANDEY
University of Allahabad.
Allahabad.

CONTENTS

LIST OF CONTRIBUTORS

Ashis Nandy
Centre for the Study of Developing Societies, Delhi

Yoganand Sinha
U. G. C. Centre of Advanced Study in Psychology, Allahabad University. Allahabad

Ype H. Poortinga
Tilburg University, The Netherlands

Forrest B. Tyler
Department of Psychology, University of Maryland, College Park, Maryland, U.S.A.

Janak Pandey
U.G.C. Centre of Advanced Study in Psychology, Allahabad University, Allahabad

Sibesh Bhattacharya
Ancient History Department, University of Allahabad, Allahabad

Om Prakash
Ancient History Department, University of Allahabad,
Allahabad

Alok Rai
Department of English, University of Allahabad,
Allahabad

S. Radhakrishnan
Indian Council of Social Science Research,
New Delhi

INTRODUCTION

The desire to understand reality and to convey to others one's understanding is probably as old as philosophy itself. The common man takes his "reality" and his "knowledge" for granted, unless he gets into some sort of problem. Quite often, the common man does get in problems because his perceived reality does not always correspond with the objective reality. The external world exists independently of the common man's perception. The gap between perceived reality and objective reality is a matter of concern for the social and other sciences. Our present concern is primarily limited to perception and understanding of social reality.

The social sciences, with varied perspectives and methods, attempt to systematize knowledge regarding the society, the individual, and various interactional products of the two to achieve unbiased knowledge about the various aspects of social reality. Before, going in some detail, we may begin with some simple questions: What is social reality? How does one know social reality? How do the social sciences construct social reality? Is there any gap between the way social reality exists and the way it is constructed in the social science? If there are such gaps, then how can they be accounted for and overcome in the process of scientific understanding? As we have noted earlier, these are not new questions.

In their systematic analysis of the subject, Berger and Luckman (1966) suggest that ".......reality is socially constructed and the sociology of knowledge must analyse the processes in which this occurs" (p. 1). We may consider the way reality is viewed by a common man, by a philosopher, and by a social scientist. Generally speaking, for a man in the street, the world in which he lives is real to him. He knows fairly well about the characteristics of the world around him. The philosopher, however, does raise some puzzling questions regarding various aspects of "reality" and "knowledge". The philosopher accepts nothing for granted like a common man and attempts to differentiate between valid and invalid assertion about the world. According to Berger and Luckman (1966) the social scientists' understanding of "social reality" and "knowledge" is between the common man and that of the philosopher.

The sociology of the knowledge perspective supports the contention that "reality" and "knowledge" both are heavily based on the social context. Social facts do not operate in a vacuum, but are influenced by the existential conditions. Berger and Luckman (1966) argue that "...a 'sociology of knowledge' will have to deal not only with the empirical variety of 'knowledge' in human societies, but also with the process by which any body of 'knowledge'comes to be basically established as 'reality'" (P. 3). It is important to understand what people "know" as "reality" in their everyday lives.

Thus, the social sciences must attempt to understand the social construction of reality. Some other sociologists of knowledge like Mannheim (1936) and Scheler (1960) are also of the view that the socio-cultural context influences perception, understanding, as well as the pursuit of knowledge. Man acts within contextual situation, where he undergoes transformations in keeping with its historico-cultural evolution. His activities are tied together through their existential cnditions. Man is not an abstract being; he is concretized in a contextual situation. Kurt Lewin's (1951) field theory analysis at times may seem that the explanation of an event depends only on the elements of the field at the time when it occurs. When Lewin formulated his principle of contemporaneity, he sought to emphasize only those aspects more directly linked to the present ("immediate") factor, but it does not necessarily follow that he was unaware that past ("mediate") factors contributed to make the event happen. The field theory aims to grasp social phenomena in their existential reality, where man appears as an agent, with some limited capacity to control his situational factors. As science develops, we find that aspects of social reality once considered accidental, become possible to be understood under the existential determination.

We may consider to examine some aspects of perception of reality in everyday life. The phenomenological analysis is probably the most suitable method to clarify the processes involved in perception and understanding of social world. The process of consciousness gets involved in one's perception. Different objects, aspects, incidents enter consciousness and they represent different levels of reality. Thus, an individual experiences multiple realities in his everyday life. For examples, an individual may perceive various aspects of the realities related to social, economic, and political lives. An individual also continually interacts and communicates with others and comes to realize that his natural attitudes to this world is quite similar to others' attitudes. Gradually, he also discovers similarities and differences with others in perceptions of a variety of aspects of the world. The knowledge one shares with others normally, thus, becomes knowledge of everyday life. According to Berger and Luckman (1966) such reality "of everyday life is taken for granted as reality". As it is obvious, knowledge of everyday life is determined by pragmatic interests of individuals and their general positions in the society to which they belong.

Berger and Luckman (1966) further suggest that like natural phenomena, social phenomena (social order, institutions, social formations) are like objective reality. Since social institutions exist as external reality, they can not be understood by an individual through introspection. So, we can grasp and understand social reality only by going out and learning about them. Again, the social world is a reality produced by man. The relationship between man and his social world, is very well described in the following words: "...the relationship between man the producer, and the social world, his product, is and remains a dilectical one. That is, man (not, of course, in isolation but in his collectivities) and his social world interact with each other. The product acts back upon the producer. Externalization and objectivation are moments in a continuing dilectical process" (p. 57, Berger & Luckman, 1966).

A number of other social scientists have explained the complex dialectical processes which exist between men and society including the Marxian views about such processes. For example, Joachim Israel (1978) while interpreting the Marxian views comments that "...society is the totality of social relations. Thus, man is produced as man by being a subject as well as an object in the network of social relations. That he is a subject means that he actively produced these relations. That he is an object means that he himself is produced by these relations. That he is an object means that he himself is produced by these relations" (p. 78). Israel (1978) mentions three media: work, language, and morals as suggested by Hegel to explain the means by which society and man are produced in a process of dialectical interaction .The work reflects man's dependence on nature. The mechanism of work process leads to production and reproduction of society and man.The media of language manifests man's dependence on other men and it makes social interactions possible. Morals, intimately interwoven with work and language, manifest man's dependence on common goals and the means of reaching them. Society is composed of processes and objectified conditions. It is the totality of ongoing interpersonal relations. Man, a product of the society, produces it. Israel (1978) recommends strongly that this complex dialectical process must be studied by social sciences. He writes, "a social science that does not take into account the dialectics of work, language, and morals with reference to basic ontological assumptions can rarely claim of itself to be 'social' or 'science'" (p. 78, Israel, 1978).

The systematization of knowledge begins with observed data. As far as physical phenomena are concerned, we find, in general a higher degree of objectivation. The stability of their structural elements and relationships among them are found so high that their objective aspects stand out more visibly. Social phenomena, however, do not present themselves with the same objectivity. They are more intimately involved in the "active experience" of the observer, so that the apprehension of their objective aspects becomes more complex. Scheffler (1967) has discussed various issues related to objectivity in observation. According to him to avoid arbitrariness in conceptualization (theory, etc.), must be constructed independently. It seems the standard notion that observation provides objectivity to conceptions is wrong. We may consider an example of McClelland and Atkinson's (1948) experiment. They studied the effect of hunger upon the images projected by subjects on to a blank screen. After a preliminary phase in which faint images were actually shown on the screen, the experimenters exposed blanks but asked for a description of the things shown. They found that the subjects gave food related responses. The size of imagined food objects increased with the increase in hunger. Thus, lesson of such findings and everyday experience seems to be that motivation, mental sets, and schemata can exercise a striking influence on an individual' contents of perception, thoughts, and understanding.

At this juncture, we may mention the developments in social psychology related to attribution theory or approach. The attribution approach is concerned with the issues like how individuals perceive and explain their own and other persons' actions. The attribution theory has developed from an emphasis on the everyday ordinary explanation of interpersonal events (Heider, 1958; Jones & Davis, 1965; Kelley, 1967). According to attribution theorists, a common goal of this approach is of understanding how individuals make causal explanations for social events, attributing causality to themselves, their fellow humans, or to physical forces in the environment. Of the last two decades, an enormous amount of research activities and data suggest that attribution of causality is determined by several factors associated with an individual's perspective. For example, actor and observer differ in their attribution of success and failure. The observer generally attributes internal factors for failure and external factors for success of an actor. However, he attributes internal factors for his success and external factors for his failure. Jones and Nisbett (1972) provide an account of differences in attribution on the basis of differences in the information available to the two people and to their different perceptual viewpoints. The actor knows more about history of action and other things around him. The observer does not know the background to the action and concentrates more on the performer than anything else. In brief, the attribution theory implicates that individuals may differ in their perspectives leading to varied perceptions of a social phenomena. For example, in our research on attribution of causality to poverty, we found that subjects with left and right political ideologies differed significantly (Pandey, Sinha, Prakash, & Tripathi, 1982). What is perceived by an individual is important because it determines his actions. In their recent work, Pandey and Singh (1985) report that perceived poverty determines behavior and coping with the economic deprivation. We may support Berger and Luckman's (1966) suggestion for the need to understand the process which operates in common man's construction of social reality to enable ourselves for a better understanding of his (common man's) action in his social context.

The empirical scientific work has received greater attention for theory building and laws in social sciences. Historically, this has been a reaction against the inadequacies of armchair theorizing. Some philosophers of science have stressed examination of the actual procedure of scientists to provide general interpretation of the history of these procedures. For example, Kuhn (1962) suggests that the history of science is a succession of "paradigms" or "disciplinary matrix". Persons with common scientific interests and training share various elements of "paradigms" and these persons constitute what Kuhn calls "scientific community". Adoption of a "paradigm" is called by Kuhn as a period of "normal science". According to Kuhn, each normal science period is terminated to overcome the difficulties that preclude continued work on the line of a paradigm, and is ultimately followed by adoption of a new paradigm. Thus, Kuhn's thesis is for "revolutionary" nature of change from one paradigm to succeeding one. These drastic changes adopted and accepted by the scientific community have been called the path of the scientific revolution. Absence of changes in paradigm may become a hindrance in the development of a science. So, Kuhn suggests that when the particular framework has largely exhausted the explanatory potentials, then it is time for change leading to adoption of another framework, a new paradigm. Probably, in terms of Kuhn's analysis, some of the social sciences are at the "pre-paradigm stage". When a potential science does not have fully viable frameworks, then it is called a science with "pre-paradigm stage". The scientists who works in a preparadigm field does not only delineate a particular perspective toward reality, but also competes with the layman's explanations and their antiprofessionalism . For example, laymen point out crushing real problems of our society such as inequality and discrimination, and they also claim that solutions of these problems are fairly clear to anyone with eyes, ears, and a human heart. However, they do recognize that these problems are of social sciences involving history, economics, sociology, and social psychology. The social scientists with their disciplinary background need to delineate the real issues, develop theories and provide practical strategies to help cope with these crushing problems. This helps the scientists to earn the layman's confidence.

To describe the nature of science, the terms "static" and "dynamic" have been used. Science as "static" consists in achieved knowledge of truth, and indicates the present interconnected set of principles, laws, and theories. According to the "dynamic" view, science is an activity of exploration continuing indefinitely. Particularly for the social sciences dynamic view is important as these disciplines deal with highly dynamic ever changing social phenomena and realities.

JANAK PANDEY

REFERENCES

Berger, P.L., & Luckmann, T. (1966). *The social construction of reality*. New York: Doubleday & Co., Inc.

Heider, F. (1958). *The psychology of interpersonal relations*. New York: Wiley.

Israel, J. (1978). Remarks concerning epistemological problems of objectivity in the social sciences. In R.A. Jones (Ed.), *Research in sociology of knowledge, sciences and art* (Vol. 1). Greenwich, CT: Jai Press, Inc.

Jones, E.E. & Davis, K.E. (1965). From acts to disposition: The attribution process in person perception.l In L. Berkowitz (Ed.), *Advances in experimental social psychology* (Vol. 2). New York: Academic Press.

Jones, E.E., & Nisbett, R.E. (1972). The actor and the observer: Divergent perceptions of the causes of behavior. In E.E. Jones et al. (Eds.) *Attribution: Perceiving the causes of behavior*. Morristown, NJ: General Learning Press.

Kelley, H.H. (1967). Attribution theory in social psychology. In D. Levine (Ed.), *Nebraska Symposium on Motivation* (Vol. 15). Lincoln: University of Nebraska

Press.

Kuhn, T.S. (1962). *The structure of scientic revolutions*. Chicago: Chicago University Press.

Lewin, K . (1951). *Field theory and social science*. New York: Harper.

Manheim, K. (1936). *Ideology and utopia*. London: Routledge & Kegan Paul.

McClelland, D.C., & Atkinson, J.W. (1948). The projective expression of needs: The effect of different intensities of hunger drive on perception. *Journal of Psychology*, **25**, 205-222.

Pandey, J., Sinha, Y., Prakash, A., & Tripathi, R.C. (1982). Right-left political ideologies and attribution of the causes of poverty. *European Journal of Social Psychology*, **12**, 327-331.

Pandey, J., & Singh, A.K. (1985). Social psychological responses to perceived and objective indicators of poverty in India. In I.R. Lagunes & Y. H. Poortinga (Eds.), *From different perspective: Studies of behavior across cultures*. Lisse: Swets & Zeitlinger B.V.

Scheffler, I. (1967). *Science and subjectivity*. New York: The Boobs-Merrill Co., Inc.

Scheler, M. (1960). *Die wissensformen und die gesellschaft*. Bern: Francke.

ONE

Ashis Nandy

SCIENCE IN UTOPIA EQUITY, PLURALITY AND OPENNESS

I

Science, particularly modern science, is no longer the greatest adventure of all. Not even for many of its dutiful practitioners. Even to many of the faithful, science is now mainly a vested interest, a commodity, a profession or, if the faithful are also given to self-denying patriotism, a national property.

Also in decline is the grandeur of science which reached its zenith in the forties and fifties of this century, overriding the anxieties triggered by the scientific marvels produced by the two world wars. The scientists no longer seem destined to win a world; they seem determined to lose one, the only one available to us at the moment. Though a part of the laity and some of the priestly classes in the modern world-especially that part of it which can be called the third world scientific establishment-continue to applaud sportingly the modern scientific worldview, to the sensitive scientists and the informed public that applause is frequently an embarrassment.

These doubts about science have come about in the 'wrong' way. To those exposed to the full power of science, the doubts have come partly from the growing awareness of the dominance of modern science at the global plane. The ideological support to science now rarely invokes the imagery so popular only forty years ago, the imagery of modern science as the self-expression of a dissenting minority, fighting the anti-scientific attitudes of the majority. Modern science, it is now obvious, has won its battle against its enemies; its concepts of rationality and epistemology now rule the world. Concurrently, though more slowly, we are becoming aware that the imperial dominance of modern science has already reduced most of us to a new state of subjecthood. We may be the citizens of the freest of polities, but we remain a part of a new periphery as the laity of science. As the impersonal structures of the scientific worldview brings newer and newer areas under its suzerainty, we are becoming conscious of being deprived of something irreplaceable and priceless which, paradoxically, we have already half-forgotten to value: our right as individuals to define the world around us and our right as individuals to declare some areas of life as off-limits to the collectivity. However, the skepticism this awareness of a new servitude has produced, while rightly stressing the role of science as a system of power, unjustly glosses over science as a system of knowledge. There is, thus, much talk about parts of the world being deprived of the fruits of modern science and there is a new awareness of the dangerous byproducts of modern science. Both the social relations and the applications of science have also come under attack. But there is little or no awareness in the non-western world of the new self-image of man which modern science has endorsed or of the new ethics and the world image it has spawned. Yet it is at that plane that science seeks to 'legitimately' homogenise the world and destroy the alternative world images as socially non-free, oppressive and-the expression is Max Weber's-'magicalising'.

In those deprived of the 'full benefits' of modern science, the recent doubts about science have arisen more directly from the growing disenchantment with modern technology. For many, modern technology is now unable to deliver the goods and this inability has suddenly made its role in human violence and exploitation more conspicuous. As a supine nature and technologised human nature face us in large parts of the world, modern man, like Mary Shelley's misunderstood pathetic monster, has turned against his mentor: modern technology and, what he sees as its adjunct, modern science. There is certainly some justification for this perception.

Since about the industrial revolution, science has been claiming credit for the technological innovations that have underwritten the modern world, even though many influential historians of science and technology have continued to say that the career lines of science and technology have been, for the most part, different. Now this claim is coming home to roost. When science and technology were clearly separable, the culture of modern science denied that separation for purposes of legitimising science by claiming the technological achievements as scientific. Now that modern science and technology are more intimately linked, the culture of modern science seeks to deny that link. As the formidable edifice of modern technology is threatened by the growing hostility against it for what it has done and for what it has allowed mankind to do to itself, modern science has begun to wriggle out of its self-assumed role as the father of modern technology. There may be poetic justice in this reversal of roles, but the result is that the recent attacks on science-as-technology remain as partial as some of the early eulogies of science-as-technology. They are founded on what science can do, not on what it is.

Can science be rescued from this deserved approbation as an adjunct of modern technology and assessed as a system of social knowledge? Can assessments of science go beyond criticisms of self-interested scientists and of violent, ecocidal, psychopathic applications of science? Can we re-examine the basic values of science to see where they have gone wrong and envision an alternative culture of science with an alternative normative framework? We cannot even begin to answer these question until we analyse the principles of hierarchy and authority which govern the present culture of science and unless we recognise that these principles derive strength from some of the basic ethical and cognitive assumptions of modern science.

II

The most totalising element of modern science is its inability to recognise itself as one of the many traditions of science. Though even scientists like Peter Medawar have argued that modern science itself includes diverse traditions, that reality has never been a part of the self-image of the scientists. They are even less willing to include within the estate of science the non-modern traditions of science. Technically modern science does recognise two other forms of science: classical science and traditional non-western sciences, what the anthropologists call ethnosciences. The former is seen as the traditional science of the west and as a no-longer-surviving progenitor of modern western science; the latter as the still-surviving poor cousins of modern science. Both classical and ethnosciences are also respected. The former is respected as a pioneering effort; the latter as tolerable approximations of science, which have, regrettably, failed to live upto the tough, mean, dirty but nevertheless real scientific world of falsifiablity, rationality, empiricism and operationalism.

However, neither the classical nor the traditional sciences are respected as competing cultures of science having their own epistemologies and ethics. They are seen as tributaries to the great river called modern science. Whatever good there was in classical science, the argument goes, is already there in modern science; whatever good there might be in the traditional sciences can be gradually incorporated in modern science as our anthropological knowledge of the non-western sciences improves. Modern science, it seems, grudgingly accepts cultural plurality in the world of science but only to the extent it can be fitted into a hierarchy.

This hierarchy is legitimised by the principles of universality and cumulation. Modern science, the principles say, because it is universal and whatever is prior in time in the world of science becomes wholly superfluous because it is incorporated in whatever is subsequent. If something is universal and cumulative–and allegedly modern science is nothing but a structure of universal, cumulative rationality–alternatives to it have the right to exist but not as alternative systems of science. And whatever is prior in such a system remains important only for the historians of the system. Such a view is a by-product of the view which sees science as a process through which we move closer to the reality of nature. If there is a real nature wholly outside human subjectivity and if different scientific theories are competing to approximate that reality, the argument goes, there has to be some theories, in fact one theory, which is objectively better than all the rest. Once such a definition of science is accepted, it obviously means that all earlier sciences are not merely different from the later sciences but also inferior to and substitutable by their successors.

Today, the unthinkable is being thought. First of all, the belief that science is a pure product of human cognition is in recession. The very fact that we discuss and debate science planning and technological R&D is an indicator of the shared belief that, left to the 'scientific temper' of the scientists, the scientific estate will produce a pattern of scientific creativity which will not be compact with human reason of ethics. True, the culture and philosophy of modern science has sold us the idea that science has such incredibly powerful self-corrective mechanisms that, in the long run, the progress of science reflects fully the strength, purity and creative power of human intellect. But, even at that plane, an increasing mass of data and insights have begun to suggest that the text of science, in addition to its context, is 'distorted' by long-term cultural and psychological forces. It is a misfortune of the votaries of modern science that they are caught in an impossible situation: modern science itself has produced scientific evidence to show that it is not an uncontaminated, rational, acultural enterprise. Today it seems fairly obvious that, even if one takes the longest of views and the strictest of empirical criteria, the existing profile of scientific knowledge is not the profile one would obtain if there were no cultural and non-cognitive determinants of science.

This is only a short step from the admission that modern science carries its moral codes within its text, not only in its application or in its cultural and organisational context. It is the ideology of modern science which does not permit modern scientists to recognise this nexus. They have to see their texts as uncontaminated and the text of others as contaminated. (It is not a very open question whether a science with such a self-image can be receptive to other ethnic sciences from different periods of time or fair to knowledge produced by alternative systems of science.)

If the doctrines of universality and cumulation are jettisoned, the dominant image of classical science in the west may or may not change. But it will surely change the images of the surviving traditions of science in other parts of the world. Certainly if you accept modern science as only an ethnoscience which has, with the help of its political and economic power, cornered other ethnosciences and assumed the role of the only universal science, you challenge the basics of the existing culture of science. Such a challenge implies that modern science can be assayed and criticised not as the science, but as the ethnoscience of the modern west, 'traditionalised' over the last four hundred years or so as one of the immutables of life. The assumptions that it is absolutely universal and perfectly cumulative can then be seen as the unique characteristics of the western ethnoscience called modern science. No more do they remain the *sine quanon* of the only valid science which must one day supplant all other sciences, if necessary by incorporating all their good points, relevant data and valid insights. They become the cultural features of a particular kind of science.

In addition to those elements in the self-image of the modern scientist which underwrite the low status of classical and ethnic sciences, the political power of modern science is legitimised by two other normative principles. These principles, both of which crucially determine the relationship between modern and non-modern sciences, are remarkably similar to the values associated with modern west's version of Christianity.

The first of the principles is the clear separation–as an aid to objectivity–between 'we' and 'they', between the subjects and the objects of science and history, and between the chosen and the pagan or the heathen. The separation parallels some other well-known oppositions. Everybody knows that expressions such as irrational or superstitious are choice abuses within the modern scientific world view and the fear of the nonrational, the insane, the mythic or the subjective are endorsed by the post-Enlightenment ideas about the new demons of mankind. In the culture of modern science, these separations are legitimised not in terms of a perceived 'natural' ordering of peoples but in terms of 'unnatural' ordering produced by some savages who are vicious enough to be anti-science or foolish enough not to seek the grace of modern science. This allows modern science to be ruthless towards all those not subscribing to its faith and towards all systems not accepting its dominance. The 'we' and 'they' here are extended to also those who distinguish between the 'we' and the 'they', and those who do not. The 'they' who accept such separation then become honorary or second-class 'we'.

The principle of proselytisation follows from the principle of separation. The modern scientific worldview is not complete unless it includes a clarion call to greater scientific spirit and an attempt to bring more areas of life under science. Much of the hostility science has generated in the occident since the eighteenth century and in the Orient since the nineteenth has been due to this drive for totalisation. Often enough, even in enthusiasts of modern science like H.G. Wells, there has been a vague resentment that modern science is one institution which seems infinite in its scope as well as ambition. At least some of his novels recognise that whereas modern science believes its theories have limited application, it imputes to itself, as a system, limitless applicability.

It is this totalism which has made modern science a dependable ally of authoritarianism in this century. More than destructive technology it is the internal structure of science which is a threat to human survival. The declared values of science, so well-summarised by Karl Popper and Robert Merton,[2] have little to do with its operational principles. As Ian Mitroff[3] seems to show, in everyday science the Mertonian values are mostly supplanted by a set of anti-values –Merton himself recognises their presence and calls them counter-norms–which could be faithfully represented by the antonyms of the former. Actually, the belief that its declared values guide everyday science is itself a major source of mystification through science. The confusion between values-as-ideals and values-as-constructions-from-action is a major plank in the culture of modern science and an important reason for the social insensitivity and simple-minded missionarism of its practitioners. That is why the principle of hierarchy which modern science applies to alternative traditions of science has been constantly projected outwards into the society as the hierarchy between the scientist and the layman and between science and other systems of knowledge. What an ethnoscience is to modern science, the layman or the non-modern scientist is to the scientist: a source material, a subject of research and experimentation, and an earlier stage of the scientist's own history of growth.

The two hierarchies–that between the scientists and the laity and that between the modern and the nonmodern sciences–have to be ensured through secular power. Many have worried about the tendency of modern science to move close to political power and to become the latter's hand-maiden. The anguished protest by a number of eminent scientists against this nexus has been become a major cultural symbol of our times. Yet this nexus between modern science and secular power is inevitable. Through all the sloganeering and public relations of modern science establishment one linkage now emerges clearer than ever. It is not so much that ill-motivated politicians, war-mongers or multinational corporations mis-use modern science: it is rather that modern scientists, discovering a natural compatibility of interests, 'correctly' and 'rationally' use the imperial structures in the world of political economy. Unless modern science is close to political power it cannot maintain its present internal structure and its hegemony in the world of knowledge.[4] (The medieval clash between the church and the scientists in Europe–regularly remembered in the myths around which the self-image of the modern scientist is built–can also be read as a struggle between the church and modern science to have greater control and greater access to state power and over the right to have a monopoly over the cosmology of western Christendom. Whatever pluralities survived after science won its battle against the church, more or less ended in the nineteenth century, when science truly became a profession. Strangely, after the relativisation of absolute space and absolute time in the Post-Einsteinian world, when the heliocentric and geocentric cosmologies have equal 'truth' values, whatever be their standing in terms of the principles of aesthetics and parsimony, it is the church which comes out better from 'history'. It at least pleaded for the acceptance of theory-as-hypothesis as opposed to Galileo who 'courageously' pleaded for the acceptance of the principle of theory-as-truth.)

The basis of modern scientific ethics has been rationalism postrenaissance humanism. The norms they have given the scientists have worked as internal checks and as self-corrective devices for about two centuries. With closer bonds developing between science, technology and industrialism since the last century, with science becoming increasingly organised and management-oriented, these norms have become totally inadequate. The monolythic rationalism modern science vends and the unthinking homocentrism which passes for humanism in the popular ideology of modern science have both become positive menaces to the human civilisation and to the very survival of the human species. However, while there is widespread discomfort about these norms and some awareness of their inadequacy, neither the discomfort nor the awareness has produced internal criticisms which could be considered basic. But for a few exceptions, the 'normal' scientists, faced with a moral crisis, have mostly reiterated what they have learnt to see as the eternal verities of science. One of these verities is the hierarchy of disciplines, linked to a subtheory of scientific progress.

I allude to the line drawn between, what J.R. Ravetz[5] calls, the mature and the immature sciences and what Thomas Kuhn, in another context, calls paradigmatic and preparadigmatic sciences. This is a dichotomy which underlies nearly all modern writings on the history and sociology of science and Ravetz only neatly restates an old classificatory, principle. The mature sciences, according to this classification, are mostly those which have 'arrived' as proper sciences (such as physics and biology); immature are those which have not allegedly 'made it' (such as sociology and political science). The immature sciences are expected, over time, to approximate the mature sciences in content as well as context and, thus, attain more respectability.

This subtheory of scientific progress–and the all-round search for certitude in our times–has meant the undervaluation of sciences which can provide sharp internal criticisms from within the culture of science, by being sciences of cultural norms and social evaluations. Today, while the social relationships and technological payoffs of the mature sciences are open to criticism, their basic axioms are not. Simultaneously, those who deal with the contents of these sciences have been given a virtually free hand to define the social responsibility of the scientists. As a result, the 'normal' scientists have a bigger say on the culture or ethics of science than do the outsiders or victims directly concerned with or affected by science. According to these 'normal' scientists, the scientific estate does not have to share responsibility–with advanced capitalism, multinational corporations, twentieth century authoritarianism, or for that matter with any of the popular villains–for the role of science in human suffering. The scientists can, however, take full responsibility for the role of science in human happiness. Whoever will give credit to the Weimer republic or to American capitalism for producing or nurturing the theory of relativity; Einstein gets the full credit for it. Who remembers the scientists who discovered the gas pellets used in the Nazi extermination camps; the Third Reich and the German industrialists get the full blame for it.

The hierarchy of mature and immature sciences also serves a large purpose which Abraham Maslow was one of the first to identify. It allows one to identify science with completed knowledge. To make his point Maslow says:

> '... there are two hierarchies of esteem in science.... One the hierarchy of well organized knowledge; the other is the hierarchy of importance of the questions one chooses to work with. It is the ones that choose to work with the crucial, unsolved, human questions, who have taken on their shoulders the fate of mankind.'[6]

Thanks to the idea of maturity of science, it is the first hierarchy which dominates the culture of science and marginalises the second. By doing so, it not merely externs philosophy and humanistic studies from the realm of science; it takes out of science possible sources of internal criticism which might help create a new science which would see itself simultaneously as a science of nature and as a science of social consciousness or–it comes to the same thing–as a philosophy of nature as well as of human nature.

An alternative vision of knowledge must recognise these limits of modern science and begin by revaluing some of the 'pre-scientific' worldviews which modern science has sought to supplant in the name of greater power over the futures of nature as well as of human nature. Probably the very fact that some of the sciences not recognised by modern science lived and live by rejecting these values of modern science, has something to tell to us about their possible uses as critiques of and alternatives to–aspects of modern science. In the second half of the twentieth century we must recognise not only the manifest, explicit criticisms of modern science in the modern sector but also the latent, implicit criticism of it in the beings of alternative traditions of science and in nonmodern life-styles.

Many accounts of ethnosciences today are available. They range from the mystical to the highly practical, from the Navaho plant classification to the ethnopsychiatries of African faith-healers, from the biofeedback-oriented yogic self-explorations to the ayurvedic science of mind-body system. Content-wise too the ethnosciences are diverse; they range from the mechanomorphic and man-as-the-master-of-nature-oriented to the pacifist and non-interventionist. In fact, there is no reason to disbelieve that there are ethnosciences at some less accessible corners of the world which share the basic assumptions of the ethnoscience which we prefer to call modern science. (Exactly as there are old cultures which beautifully fit in with the modern world. According to some, such overlaps prove the greatness of such cultures; according to others, it could also be a matter of some concern.

I am not preparing the ground for a total defence of the non-modern sciences as the sole design of an alternative culture of science, but for a critical defence of them as marginalised systems which carry intimations of an alternative relationship between science and society. This defence must begin with the awareness that, despite their basic difference, traditional sciences do have in common their political position in the world of knowledge. This position is one of powerlessness, peripherality and inacessibility. Thuds, a reaffirmation of traditional sciences may not take us out of the present crisis of science, but it can certainly help widen our choices in the matter of the future of science.

Such plurality need not fragment scientific knowledge. On the contrary, meaningful cohesion in a democratic culture of science is possible only on the basis of a continuous dialogue among the various traditions of science and on the basis of equality, autonomy and dignity of the participant sciences in that dialogue. The dialogue may even lead to a culturally non-relativistic perception that some ethnosciences are limited in scope–that is, it may lead to a new critique of the ethnosciences, too. An understanding of the limits and languages of the different traditions of science–and locating the concept of equality among sciences outside the compass of cultural relativism–allows for cultural criticism and evaluation of the cosmologies in which the various sciences are embedded. Equality here implies equal cognitive respect for each ethnic construction of knowledge as an endeavour carrying the codes of its environment. It does not imply unconditional moral acceptance of all sciences.

Likewise, autonomy does not merely mean absence of dominance by the culture of modern science. It also means wider legitimacy for all efforts to construct inter-translatable languages for the ethno-sciences so that they can communicate with each other and with modern science without being swept of their feet. And the dignity I speak of is the dignity that has been taken away from all knowledge systems except the modern one. Henryk Skolimowski has said that science at one time was an embodiment of human dignity; it has become now a disgrace to human dignity. One could add that modern science has now also become a means of depriving large parts of the world of their dignity. To restore that dignity, one must affirm that if the non-modern sciences are valuable, it is not because they can be translated into the language of modern science and made readable; nor because some aspects of the non-modern sciences can be interpreted as 'rational' when seen as an aspect of a folk science surviving in a special habitat at the periphery of the world; nor even because they sometimes have a clear practical dimension (as in the case of acupuncture) or because they fit in with the transient concerns of the modern west (as in the case of Zen psychology). The dignity of the ethnosciences can be restored only when we alter our scientific worldview to accommodate them in it, at least partly on their own terms.[7]

III

The modern scientist's definition of his own freedom is simple: he must be allowed to go where his science takes him. This definition is based on the assumption that the scientific imagination of the scientist, if given free play and total autonomy and if liberated from the constraints of the nonscientific self of the scientist, would be both creative and ethical. The last one hundred years of modern science has shown this assumption to be false. The elimination of interference by religion has not made science freer, it has only prompted the scientists to seek new authorities voluntarily. The recent history of modern science is not so much a history of the state interfering in science. it is a history of the modern scientist seeking the patronage of the state and bringing it into the core of science, either directly or through his conformity to conventional professional values. Predictably now, there is call for 'deestablishment of science'-for 'a separation, as complete as possible, between science and government in all countries'. The results are unlikely to be very different from the ones we obtained by separating science and religion. The modern scientists will only find new patrons and a new establishment to which to be allegiant. The basic problem lies elsewhere: scientists are no longer an undersocialised part of the modern society, as they once certainly were; they are now oversocialised products of the modern age. Why this voluntary servitude?

Notwithstanding propaganda, the position of the scientist in the modern society is insecure. The modern worldview has a basic contradiction built into it. On the one hand it swears by science; on the other, it denies sanction to anything which is purely aesthetic, intuitive, philosophical or non-utilitarian. I have said at the beginning that modern scientists have for long sought legitimacy as purveyors of technology. I should have said that they have been forced to do so by a society which is not science-minded but technique-oriented. Pure science in the modern west is certainly an effeminate, childish pursuit incompatible with the lifestyle of the ideal man. Less than five per cent of all scientists are engaged in it. No wonder that a large number of the psychological studies of creativity done in the fifties and sixties showed that two of the major differentiae of the creative scientist in the west were his 'femininity' and 'infantility'.

Any vision of a future science must take into account this devaluation of the scientist in a society manifestly wedded to science and build a liberating vision for him too. Earlier efforts to do so have gone in two directions. The first kind has made scientists pursue some of the old doctrines of transcendence overtly, the way Newton spent a large portion of his working time on theological pursuits (though he overtly kept these pursuits separate from his science, he was convinced that his science confirmed his theological speculations). The new version of this position is represented by those normal scientists who try to justify through their science some forms of religion, spiritualism or traditional philosophy. Popular scientists of this kind of our times are James Jeans and Fritjof Kapra, both of whom have sought and found parallels between aspects of modern science and traditional worldviews. The standard modern response to this position is to split the scientist into two: the sane, acceptable scientist and the woolly-headed, part-time mystic who has to be tolerated for the simple reason that no man is perfect. Conventional histories of science has two Newtons: one who was a great scientist and one who was a man of religion with eccentric ideas about the meanings of science. In our times a similar fate has been met by scientists who have delved into politics, social criticism or philosophy of science.

A variant of this response has sought to assess persons, ideologies, modes of experience or utopias with reference to science, allegedly to give the assessees a new dignity. For instance, some scholars and social leaders in nineteenth century India rejected much of modern science but nonetheless justified many traditional practices with the help of the science they rejected. Pre-war theosophists in Europe searched pathetically for new theories and findings of modern science compatible with their mysticism, all the while criticising modern science for its incompleteness, heartlessness and mechanomorphism. In our times, movements like the one organised around transcendental meditation claim their forms of mysticism to he the most modern and scientific of a all forms of mysticism rather than claiming them to be the best models of transcendence or the most humane forms of the occult. And to give a more academic instance, some social anthropologists have tried to show that myths are a mode of scientific discourse rather than trying to understand modern science as a form of myth. Even for its critics, modern science has become an absolute standard or a measure of truth.

The second model of liberation of scientists is marked out by the part-time efforts of many scientists to be politically and socially active. This model has so influenced the mainstream social studies of science that such studies mainly focus on the organisation, economics and academic politics of science and exclude from their scope the mind of the scientists and the politics of science as a life-style. As a result, critiques of science are separated from critiques of the scientist's professional self. So much so that if the professional life of a scientist is not touched by his activism, it goes to his credit and he is admired for remaining a 'true' scientist inspite of being politically conscious. Such a split beautifully contains the dissent of a scientist and makes it manageable on behalf of the Establishment. It reduces the politically and socially active scientist to the stature of an ornamental dissenter within the system, apart from fracturing both human knowledge and selfhood. Such activism becomes a rationalisation-in Freud's sense of the term-of everyday professional life and of conformity to the conventional values of science.

Any design for the liberation of the scientist must begin with an attack, not only on his class position or social location, but also on the enveloping, possessive, hold of culture of modern science on him. Liberating knowledge must represent a continuity between self-awareness and awareness of the world, and between commitment to science as a construction of truth and science as a mythography. Such knowledge cannot but believe in science as a form of critical consciousness which, like any other system of critical knowledge, skeptically examines existing 'truths' to show that they are not the truths they are believed to be. (As a definition of science-and, by implication, of scientists-this of course bears a similarity to Ananda Coomaraswamy's definition of traditional art as iconoclasm). It is this negative value of science which interrelates as well as cuts across cultures and schools of science. This approach recognises that science is a quality of thinking and a form of aesthetics, rather than a thing or a collection of things, material or otherwise. It is based on the faith that science as a quality of thinking can be enriched by involving the scientific and the non-scientific selves of the scientist, not by helping him to split himself into a scientist and a human being.

NOTES

1. This issue has been discussed in some detail in Ashis Nandy, 'Science, Authoritarianism and Culture: on the Scope and Limits of Isolation Outside the Clinic', M.N. Roy Memorial Address, New Delhi, March 1980, published in *Seminar*, May 1981, (261).
2. Karl Popper, *Refutations and Conjectures* (London: Routledge, 1963), Chapter 1, and Robert Merton's *Social Theory and Social Structure* (Glencoe: Free Press, 1957).
3. Ian Mitroff, *The Subjective Side of Science*, (Amsterdam: Elsevier, 1974).
4. The first part of the argument is compatible with that made by Herbert J. Bernstein, 'Idols of Modern Science and the Reconstruction of Knowledge', *Journal of Social Reconstruction*, 1980, 1, pp. 27-56, Bernstein says that modern science has never cared to point out that since the relativisation of

space in the modern physics, the shift from the Ptolemaic to Copernician universe no longer looks like a shift from falsity to truth but from faith to the human-based criterion of simplicity. On the nature of the conflict between church and state, A.K. Saran's works have directed me to Owen Barfield, *Saving the Appearances: A Study in Idolatry* (London: Faber and Faber, 1957).

5. J.R. Ravetz, *Scientific Knowledge and its Social Problems* (Harmondsworth: Penguin Books, 1973); T.S. Kuhn, *The Structure of Scientific Revolutions* (Chicago: University of Chicago, 1962). Analogous and to some extent overlapping classifications are those between toughminded and softminded psychology, made by H.J. Eysenck, and between science and pseudo-science, made by Peter Medawar.
6. Abraham Maslow, 'The Desacralization and the Resacralization of Science'. In *The Psychology of Science: A Reconnaisance* (Chicago: Henry Regnery, 1966), pp. 138-152, see pp. 147-148.
7. Bronowski, quoted in Bernstein, 'Idols of Modern Science', p. 38.

TWO

Yoganand Sinha

PERSPECTIVE IN HUMAN SCIENCES

Social reality,its perception and understanding have tormented mankind for time immemorial. This paper intends to trace this struggle of man, particularly within Human Science. Human Sciences are aware and systematic enquiries into man's actions, cognition, his relationship with other men, history and nature. Human Science attempts to explore processes by which man cognizes and acts in order to cope, adjust, and change the natural and social context wherein he lives. Arbitrary, as it may be, this paper begins from the birth of a human concern called Sociology of Knowledge. Sociology of Knowledge tries to show how perception, knowledge (theory) and understanding of social reality is influenced and regulated by social experience, value and locale of the observer in the social structure. In short, it "attempts to explore and understand the relationship between cognitive structure (broadly speaking) and social structure" (Buss, 1979, p.3). The central assumption is that human beings can know only a socially mediated reality. A reality constituted with the help of a complex interacting sets of social categories and symbols. The role of perspective in Human Science, hence becomes pivotal.

Perspective signifies the manner in which one looks at the world, how and what one makes out of it in ones life and thought. It has a qualitative element in the way of structuring and conceiving social reality. Perspectives, in Human Science, are systems of interacting symbols or constructs which tend to link phenomena in cause-effect relationship. Thus, it organises, defines, and directs enquiries towards phenomena. It interprets social reality and mobilieses consensus and collectively around social goals and values, legitimizes actions and projections of self images within Human Science. The human enquiry into men's action is valid and possible only because man can make his own action the object of his intentional scrutiny. Thus,. in the very inception of Human Science there is implied an identity between the "object" of study and "subject" studying it. This makes the role of perspectives even more crucial in Human Science.

Man's action is linked to his way of construing the world and is not merely an automatic mechanical reflex to stimulus world. Man transforms and confers meaning on the stimulus world and acts in relationship to his meaningful world (Berger 1974). Man acts in accordance with his interpretations, beliefs, desires and intentions. Hence, the study of man's act (Human Science) is not the study of "action perse", but the construction of it in meaningful concepts. All enquiry of man's action entails social constructs, symbolic universe or the "world of words". Constructs, in turn, are formed by a process in which the essentials are preserved and non-essentials are rejected. The question of what is essential or non-essential is a matter which is closely linked to "perspectives". In other words, the capacity of man and Human Science to transform into meaningful constructs, their object of study, are theoretically limitless. The ways of construing the world are, however, regulated by the perspectives used to view the world. Hence the existing regularities and consistencies in construing the social world (Gergen 1982, Berger 1974). For example, Human Science, which is a social phenomena itself, seem to have a great divergence as to what the goal of study is and should be. Questions such as: what to study? how to study? why to study?, all have variegated answer. The differences in answers are not random but can be traced to historically contingent conceptual structures and meaning systems. These differences can be traced to divergence of interests and perspectives of different classes and groups existing in any modern society wherein social sciences occur. The goals and constructs of Human Science enquiry still offend classes and group interests, unlike those of Natural Science, Thus, enquiries in Human Science originate from fundamentally different prospectives, consider different aspects as essential for Human Science, and construct the nomothetic net-work differently, culminating in an inherent lack of consensual objectivity. This lack of consensus on both the meaning of constructs and their operational definition is neither a weakness of an individual researcher nor the immaturity of the discipline (Human Science) as alluded by Durkheim (1954)... "The rule requires that the sociologist assume the same state of mind as physicists, chemists and physiologists when they get involved in a still unexplored area of their scientific domain. But sociology is far from having arrived at this degree of intellectual maturity" (p.xiv). It is contended, that there exists a fundamental difference between majority of Human Science phenomena, as opposed to Natural Science phenomena. Hence, no matter how well one applied the Cartesian method, it does not suffice for Human Science. The very analytical components by which one looks at a phenomena are themselves influenced by perspective prior to the enquiry. The lack of objectivity is not resolved by use of "the method", rather, it exists because of the "subject-object" identity incherent in Human Science (Gergen 1982a).

Despitie the "subject-object" identity and lack of objectivity, a perspective is not completely idiosyncratic. No one persective can construct "do novo" it's object of study. It is permeated, constrained and embedded in the past, experience, language convention and social conditions which are "given" factors for the perspective. Construct within a perspective are not merely a passive simulacrum of the "given". The "given" and the "constructed" are inextricably related with one another. For example, man can be seen as subject, construing reality by his own action and at the same time as an object acted upon, influenced and recognised only with the help of language and historical social context. Man is simultaneously both the mediating subject and a part of the reality of things mediated through him. Hence, perspectives being a human phenomena, emerge and are transmuted alongwith changes in human endeavours and social conditions.

Having emphasized the importance of perspectives in Human Science, the next question which arises is, how to identify various perspectives? How does one know the perspective one from which is looking at the human world and the acts of men? One of the simplistic and naive, albeit popular and credulous answer is, to ascribe the perspective to the life events of the observes. If one knows the biography of the individual, such as where he was born, what job he did etc., one can know the perspective of the person. Without undermining the influence of such factors, one feels that such overtly "objective" criterion' for identifying perspective prevents one from uncovering the qualitative elements. More so, such a simplistic approach is bound to lead to mechanical and distorted reductionism, which ignores, the creative struggle of man in evolving a perspective. It disregards the dialectic of the human behaviour and the social context, which is an integral part of any perspective. Following Mannheim (1936). Goldmann (1970), Schultz (1962), Berger and Luckman (1966), this paper argues that perspectives can best be comprehended by paying attention to concepts presents and absent in an enquiry, to the model of thought used and the assumptions asserted. For instance, in psychology there is a range of motivational concepts which are used to explain behaviour. However, different theorists use only certain motivational concepts and ignore others, which inturn connotes their perspective. Further, the absence of certain concepts, such as detachment, from the array of motivational concepts reflects the perspective and concerns of western man. In short, one has to focus one's attention to stipulations concerning the nature of man, the nature of knowledge man can have, the nature of society if one wants to reveal and identify the qualitative elements of a perspective (Israel 1972).

These stipulations are based on fact-value claims (Tylor 1967). All these stipulations are supported by value claims and data base, Thus, it is not surprising that most hypothesis in Human Science are empirically proved and theroretically sound even while they may be mutually opposite or rwaling hypothesis. This is because in social science the facts are embedded in theoretical constructs which in turn, are embedded in perspective or epistemic presuppositions. Mere adherence to "facts" do not help when confronted with two opposing sets of stipulations, each being supported by an impressive data base and theoretical edifices. Further, the differences between two or more perspectives cannot be resolved by step-by-step logical refutation, since the debate is about premises. One can resort only to persuasion.

One set of stipulation about the nature of man, is that like the unchanging biological core, man has an"essential core" be it sexuality or power seeking or "role learning". He is historical, only in the sense that he lives to reveal this essential core. His essence is ageless. Hence, within this perspective man is seen as a product of roles played by him. His life-all his action, aspiration, hope, cognition and thinking-is seen as his efforts to learn the role and fulfil role demands, and expectation. Further he "does not only learn to act according to roles but internalises the value that one must act according to roles" Parson (1961). Hardfield (1968) going one step further tries to argue that man actually has some basic arche-typical needs which pattern his action to suit roles". In short, man is but a reflection of the essence, which is universal spanning across all division of society and differences between societies.

The subscribers to this perspective, generally ignore the questions about the nature of society. they do not normally, see any systematic relationship between nature of society and the nature of man or knowledge one can have, even though they may refer to society as full of amorphous forces giving rise to "role demands" and "role expectations", However, the best of them, following Homans Parson (1961) and (1961) do stipulate about the nature of society Concepts such as "checks and balances", clearly imply the use of mechanical analogy, equilibrium, is the cardinal concept of this model. Society is seen as counteracting all forces which tend to destabilize and establishing balance or equilibrium, more so as in a closed system. All phenomena which lead to change in the balance, arising out of conflict of interest, are seen as negative forces leading towards anthropy and disorder. All such forces are seen as problems, warranting attention and enquiry. Equilibrium, maintenance of balance are rarely, if ever, labelled as "problems" (Iserael 1972).

Similar to the mechanical model, society is sometimes seen analogous with organism. The functional interdependence of each elements of society is emphasised for the "optimum performance" and"survival of the social system". Maintenance of "law order", "pattern of interdependence" is the goal of the organismic model. Once again, the meaning of "survival of the system" is left unquestioned and amorphous, implying, that beyond the mere survival of the members, it means the survival of perpetuation of a "given" social order. The fact that both treat equilibrium or optimum performance as obvious makes the theories, studies and findings within this perspective acritical about the nature of society and the social arrangement.

In summary, this perspective, basically sees man as a role bearer. Knowledge as passive simulacrum of external given and society as mechanical or organismic. Further, any phenomena suggesting change in the given equilibrium is seen as pathological or, at best, a problem which ought to be "set right". This basic acceptance of status quo, and the construction of man as object of force rather, than as a "subject" originator of action, has lent this perspective open to positivistic and empirilistic investigation. The social theory and enquiry generated from this perspective are very impressive both in volume and scientific quality but fail to make explicit the underlying pro-status quo implications.

The other set of stipulation, sees man as a "self-creating". Man is not a fixed entity, but as an ever changing active "being" and a process which is both the bases of change and the product of change. Hence, man is the total of social relations -this is not to say that man is only an object or consequence of social relations but, that the nature of man is his relations with others and the world.G.H.Mead (1934) suggests that "a self arises only where there is a social process within which this self had its initiation . It arises within the process". This dialectical approach is a departure from the Cartesian 'position, in which difference and inequality between self and other is the basis of scientific method of knowledge. Scheib (1979 argues that the concept of universal human science cannot allow peerage and equality between subject and object of study. This distance between the social scientist and his object of study gets transmuted into inequality of status, advantages and participation. The scientist is better than those he studies, he stands to gain more from the study than those whom he studies and virtually there is no participations of those who are studied in designing and conceptualization of the study, except as respondents.

However, dialectical perspective sees man as a social phenomenon, wherein the subject (knowing man) and object (the world or society) are treated as mutually influencing each other and as equals in Praxis. Praxis understands man as an active subject constantly engaged in structuring and recognizing into meaningful totalitics its relations with world of men and nature (Hoffman 1975). The epistemological position suggested by praxis is best is best exemplified in the works of Piaget. Here, knowledge becomes an activity (Leontev 1978), a process in which a subject constructs its cognition in an active relationship with the world. "Assimilation" and "Accommodation" are constructive progresses, based upon the scheme already acquired through past relationship with the world. thus, man is seen as an autonomous beholder of alternative, but not completely independent of the world as "given" both in language convention and objective material reality.

Further, dialectical perspective views society as an ongoing process. The process model or dialectical materialist model stipulates society as "a complete multi-faced fluid interplay or of widely varying degree and intensities of association and dissociation". Here, society is seen as a continuously changing and creative process. Any reference to structure is only as a consociation between various elements of society for a given time period "as snapshots of ongoing process" (Weick, 1982). Hence, forces which bring about change are as valid a problem" as forces trying to maintain any given orders or structure. Conflict and consensus are both questioned. Man's role in society is not merely that of internalizing and maintenance of a "given" structure but also of changing it and evolving a new social arrangement or system. Thus, making it imperative to study man's act as a "whole" along with its integral component, of aspirations, intention, goals and efforts of changing himself and the world. The theories and data within this perspective are very critical of "what is", and thus, fully adher to an existence of an intimate relationship between value statement and statement of fact. That is What "ought to be" may condition by what is and vice versa" (Gergen 1982; Buss 1979).

The two perspectives cites above are not the only ones to be found in Human Science. For instance one could recognise a "conspirational perspective", which stipulates that some persons are beyond social influence and they affect history unilaterally (Israel 1972). Yet again, a lot of empirical enquireies in Human Science, particularly in psychology could be said to be ahistorical. Man is seen only as he is, here and now, and that too in terms which can be operationally measured and nothing more or less. This atomizes man almost to the extent of Dali's paintings.

Many other sets of stipulation are prevalent in Human Science. However, the two perspectives briefly described are the most coherent and consistent. More sc, others tend to fall on either sides of this "great divide" adumberated by those two perspectives. In summary, perspectives in Human Science can be recognized by scrutinising (a) the stipulations regarding the nature of man, the nature of society, the type of knowledge man can have, (b) what is considered as obvious and treated in amorphous manner, (c) what are the concepts used and what concepts are absent, and (d) the extent to which findings and theories are critical of the social order.

Once it is accepted that perspective in infused into Human Scientific theory and data, that is, once the influence of extra scientific values in scientific efforts is recognized, there arises the question about the criterion of choice between perspectives. How is one to choose between any two perspectives, each of which has an impressive theory and data to substantiate itself. It is argued here that the choice should not be a matter of either accident or individual's whims and fancy, rather, that Human Science should evolve criterion and must make this choice a deliberate act with full cognisance of responsibility entailed in such a climacteric choice.

If one was to share with Durkheim and his present day followers, the Cartesion optimism, then, one could easily evolve the criterion. Any perspective which enables one to use the natural science method would be "better". There exists, as suggested earlier, a fundamental difference between phenomena in Natural Science and those in Human Science. Further, the success of Natural Science method is to a large extent attributable to the choice of phenomena investigated by the method. Hence this simple answer is of little help in evolving a criterion in Human Science. If fact, this transfer of method from natural science to Human Science is imbued with danger as suggested by Robinson (1976)..."main danger of civilization arises from the inability of minds trained in the natural science to perceive the difference between the economic and the technical". Further, this tendency to emulate natural science method tends to predetermine the fate of Human Science, i.e. Human Sciences will be, what Natural Sciences are today. Even the most ardent advocate of the method, find such a determinism unacceptable. More so, the failure of Human Science in yielding universal law by use of natural science method is well documented. Hence, traditional cannons of "science" are not of much help evolving criterion for the choice between perspectives in human science.

Max Weber sensitive to the problem arising from the very condition and nature of Human Science, suggested that the role of Value should be accepted within Human Science. But values should intervene only in the choice of problems - (but) not in the study of it. However, fact and values, values and theory and theory and presupposition are so intimately related, that one finds that the whole of scientific conduct is suffused with values choices (McClure & Tyler 1967). Even so, Weber's acceptance of the role of value in Human Science is laudable, as values had been banished from the realm of science by positivists before him. Thus, any perspective which accepts the role and influence of (stipulation) values and focuses its enquiring attention on the relationship of values and fact is "better" than perspective which deny it and render the role of values inexplicable.

Secondly, any perspective which permits the understanding of the other perspective as a social and human phenomena, which reveals its infrastructure and vivifies the constructs by means of critical examination of other's consistency and limitation, is "better". Since, no enquiry even after making explicit its fact, value assumptions is able to see all its weakness and shortcomings, there is a need for criticism from other perspectives. This criticism is essential for the growth of Human Science. Hence, in choosing between two perspectives the one which provides the widest range of criticism of other perspective is "better". It is better and preferable than those which do not criticism other perspectives or those which accept the relativistic position that all "fact-theory" are equally true. The relativist argument is that since all theories are sometime true and since none is true for all times, all theories-facts are equally valid or invalid. Thus, there is no necessity of of a choice between theories and perspectives.

The third suggestion for the criterion of choice is the degree to which any perspective allow for and critically applies its own findings to itself A perspective which examines its own theory and evaluates its own stipulations in the light of its own finding and experience, is "better". That is to say that all method, beliefs, values and hopes, including one's basic philosophical position, are open to self criticism (Bartley 1962). Thus, self-criticism and consequent modification in the stipulations makes a perspective more dynamic and such a perspective has greater chances of approximating the dynamic social reality.

Any attempt to evolve criterion of choice between perspectives would not be viable unless one takes into consideration the individual researcher. Karl Mannheim, giving due importance to the researcher(intelligentia) suggests that human scientist is the some degree "freer" and thus, has greater responsibility. The task of the Human Scientist, is to achieve the most comprehensive approximation of social reality, and because of this, he is aware of different perspectives. More so, the necessity of scientific thought makes it impossible for him accept two mutually incompatible perspectives. Thus, his task requirements enable him to enjoy relatively greater autonomy than some other member of society. That is not to say, that his thought and synthesis do not have class, value or stipulative biases, but only to suggest that his position is of "relative independence" vis-a-vis the group to which he belongs. The Human scientist has to be aware that along with the difficulties common o all science, such as logical consistency, precision, etc., he is confronted with the difficulties arising from the highly dynamic and constructive nature of man and the phenomena he studies. Of course, this is so only if he intends to remain a scientist and not become a technician as most social paychologist have become today. Moscovici (1972) concludes that "social paychologists have done no more than operationalize question and answers which were imagined elsewhere. And thus, the work in which they are engaged is not the work of scientific analysis but that of engineering" (p.32). Moreover, the researcher has to be aware that the influence of perspective is continuous and permanent, meaning that a more acceptance of ones stipulations and its regulative influence does not solve the problem of bias. It is an every every day struggle to uncover within oneself and one's enquiry the influence of predilection, values and stipulations; a struggle to critically examine and reveal the-relationship of one's work and life, one's position in society and the social conditions of the time. Most researchers tend to avoid this uncomfortable exercise and hide behind the volume of publication or data or the security that generation to come will do the criticism. What is suggested here is self-criticism, to live and work with self criticism.

Further, Human Scientist must realise that the choice he makes between perspectives, is his responsibility and consequently so are the implications of the findings of his enquiry. That is any body who studies and more so, publishes his findings must be aware that he is acting socially and politically. His findings being inherently valuational, will subtly, if not openly favour certain patterns of conduct and influence others, they may catalize resistance, create conflict on generate solidarity. His findings are going to contribute directly and by implication to either, justification of the arrangements of society, or to criticising and debunking this arrangement, or distracting the attention from such issues of social systems (obscuratism) and, by default, sustaining the status quo (Mills 1973). Hence he must have the willingness and develop the capacity to challenge the guiding assumptions of culture, to raise fundamental questions regarding contemporary social life, to foster reconsideration of all that which is taken for granted and thereby to generate fresh alternatives for social life. At the same time he has to admit that his work is at best an approximation and valuable only until such time as its limits are pointed out, or society has undergone a change. It is precisely this "approximation" which entails choice and responsibility of choice. For, if exactness was possible or supposed one could not be held responsible for the implication of the discovery of this "exactitude". It is not surprising that a Human scientist who sees data as "the only reality" can and does argue that a social scientist has very little, if any, responsibility for the implication of his findings. However, when "approximation" is posited then one has responsibility of the implications of ones approximation, and the need to go beyond data, to accept greater responsibility. The social scientist has to constantly view and review his work with reference to the dialectic of individual society and of science society, both being intimately connected and infused in his endeavour (Buss & Royce, 1976).

The human scientist would have to spend more time, effort and energy on critically examining (a) his own values, hopes and the influences these have upon his work, (b) the social context social arrangement of power, status, etc., within which he and his work is located,(c) the impact and implications of his work on the social arrangements, (d) the various perspectives prevalent and its relationship to "historically contingent" class or interest groups in society, Further, he has to evolve criterion to chose between perspectives and do so with full awareness of the responsibility entailed in such a choice. All this he has to do, over and above the other requirement of science such as logical clarity, consistency, precision and data gathering. The overbearing presence of perspective and its influence makes human science challenging. Human science endeavour is not merely, a question of technique, skill and refined habit but a form of social commitment, of "becoming" and encountering life and social reality.

REFERENCES

Bartley, W.W., *The retreat to commitment*. New York; Knopf, 1962.

Barger, P.L., *Pyramids of sacrifice; Political ethics and social change*. Penguin Books, 1974.

Burger,P.L.& Luckman, T., *The social construction of reality*; Penguin Books, 1966.

Buss, A. *Psychology in social context*. New York; Thirington, 1979 a.

Buss, A. *dialectical psychology*, New Yor' Halsted Press, 1979 b.

Du khiem, E., *The elementary forms of religious life*. London. Allen & Unwin, 1954.

Gargen, K., *Towards transformation in social knowledge*. New York, Springer, 1982.

Gergen, K. & Gergen, M.M., Forms and function in the explanation of human conduct. In p Second (ed) *paradigms in the social science*. Beverly Hill: Sage publishers, 1882.

Goldman, L., *The human science and philosophy*. Jonathan Cape, 1970.

Hortifield, G., As quoted by J. Israil in stipulation and construction in the social science, 1968.

Hoffman, J., *Marxism and theory of rakis* New York; International Publishers, 1975.

Homans, G., *Social behabviour, Its elementary forms*. New York; Harcourt Brace, 1961.

Israel, J., Stipulation and construction in the social science. In J. Israel and H. Tajfel (ed). *The context of social psychology. A Critical Assessment*. London: Academic Press, 1972.

Kuhn, T.S., *The structure of scientific revolution*. Chicago: University of Chicago Press, 1970.

Leontev, A.N. *Activity, consciousness and personality*. New Jersey: Printice Hall, 1978.

Mannheim, K., *Ideology and utopia*. London, Routledge and Kegan Paul Ltd, 1936.

Mannhecim, K. *Essays on the Sociology of knowledge*. London: Routledge & Kegan Paul ltd, 1952.

Marx, K., *The German ideology*. London; Lawerence & Wishart, 1965

Moad, G.H. *Mind, self and society from the standpoint of social behaviourist*. Chicago: university of Chicago press, 1934

Mills, C.W. *The sociological imagination*. Penguin Books, 1973.

Moscovici, S., Society and theory in social paychology. In J. Israel and H. Tajfel (ed). *The context of social paychology : A critical assessment*, London: Academic Press, 1972.

Parson, T. Outline of the social system. *In theories of society*. Glencoe : Free Press, 1961.

Piaget, J. The stages in intellectual development of the child. *Bulletin of the Man-*

ninger Clinic 26 1962 120-128.

Robinson, D.N., *An intellectual history of paychology*. New york, McMillon. 1976.

Ring,K., Some sober questions about frivolous Values. *Journal of experimental social psychology 3.*,1976

Scheibe, K., *Mirrors, marks, lies and secrets*. New York, Praiger, 1979.

Schultz, A. *Collected papers*. The Hague: Nijhoff,1962.

McCluro, T. & Tyler, F.B., Policy decisions in science : Psychological consideration and implication for 1967 paychology. *Journal of General Psychology 77* 69-86.,

Weber, M. *The methodology of the social sciences*. New York; Free Press 1949.

Weick, K.E., Cognitive processes In organisation. *In research in organisation Behaviour*, 1979.

THREE

Ype H. Poortinga

ON ERRONEOUS PERCEPTION, POOR PREDICTION AND THE UTILITY OF APPLIED SOCIAL SCIENCE

There is substantial evidence indicating that our perception of the world does not provide us with a precise and complete representation, in the sense of a photographic record. Not only is there far more information in most environments than we can cope with, so that we miss many details, but previous experiences and preconceived notions also play an important role (e.g. Gibson, 1966). Many of these notions are embedded in our language. Undergraduate students of psychology are nowadays introduced to this insight when they learn that Eskimo use 20 different words for the variety of phenomena denoted in English with 'snow' and that Arabs have a few hundred words to describe various states and aspects of pregnancy in camels. But the importance for perception of the perceiver's organization of the world was known long before cross-cultural studies became fashionable. It was in fact a main principle of one of the earliest traditions in the systematic study of behaviour, namely Gestalt psychology (e.g. Wertheimer, 1925).

The tendency towards systematization and organization of the environment also governs our perception of other persons. According to personality researchers we tend to describe the behaviour of others in terms of so-called personality traits. These are dispositions such as honesty, aggressiveness and dominance, which presumably lead to consistency in reaction patterns across a wide range of situations. On the other hand when asked to report on our own actions, we emphasize the demands of a particular situation or our goals and intentions. In other words, I steal a leaf of bread because I am hungry, but you do it because you are a dishonest person (Jones and Nisbett, 1971).

It seems rather obvious that preconceived notions similarly influence our perception and understanding at the more encompassing level of a cultural group or country and in the wider frame of an historical perspective. About two hundred years ago the technological superiority of the West European nations was attributed to the climatic conditions of the region. A moderate climate was seen as conducive to hard work and consequent societal progress. A century later with the rise of biology and evolutionism the concept of race was frequently mentioned as a determinant of intercultural differences. Today such differences are mostly explained in terms of socio-cultural factors. For example, low socio-economic status and lack of educational opportunities rather than genetic predisposition nowadays are seen as the cause of the low scores of certain racial groups on tests of intellectual abilities (Kamin, 1974).

The shifts in explanation which have taken place in the past lead to the question what claims we can make about the validity of our contemporary knowledge. Of course, this kind of problem has been of central interest throughout the history of philosophy, but this paper will not be concerned with epistemological issues. I merely want to argue that the insights which we value, and often even cherish, are in all probability not less fallacious or incomplete than those of our predecessors which have been rejected or simply forgotten.

Let me quickly add that I do believe in progress of science, also when it comes to the explanation of social events. However, there will be little real progress if we do not take seriously the shortcomings and limitations of our work. One of these limitations I would like to elaborate, namely that scientific explanation of any kind becomes less successful as the number increases of the parameters which possibly influence the phenomena to be explained.

Social scientists tend to look with some jealously at natural scientists who achieve mathematical representation, almost error free measurement and consequent accurate prediction, or so at least it seems. Platt (1964) has used the term 'strong inference' in an article in which he mentions how the structure of DNA was discovered in a series of experiments in which with each study a wrong alternative could be eliminated and the search continued in what ultimately proved the right direction.

When it comes to the application of natural science knowledge in the form of technology, achievements are not less impressive, but their success is far more equivocal. To clarify this point I need only to refer to the generally unforeseen effects of DDT or acid rain and the extensive debates on the possible effects of changes in ozone and carbon dioxide levels in the atmosphere.

Although this is not the only possible perspective it, seems fair to argue that these examples show that the accuracy of explanation and prediction decreases as the number of contextual factors with a potential effect on the phenomenon under scrutiny increases. It may be emphasized that in themselves the processes involved need not be so complex as to baffle the human mind. In random number generation fairly simple algebraic procedures are used. Nevertheless, they quickly lead to a level of complexity which makes the resulting series of numbers indistinguishable from 'random' sequences.

In psychology there are also achievements which appear to be part of an accumulating body of knowledge and which are unlikely to be refuted in the future. They are mainly found in the area of experimental psychology where the available methodology allows for the study of the relevant phenomena in isolation, or at least under controlled conditions. Elementary learning principles such as conditioning and contingent reinforcement form the most obvious examples (Catania, 1979). Dogs can be made to salivate and pigeons can learn to distinguish between targets at the whims of a psychologist. Human - machine interaction systems in which results from research on perception and motor skills are applied can also be mentioned. Probably I can go even further. The work of Harlow (e.g. Harlow and Zimmerman 1959) with rhesus monkeys is likely to remain part of a more permanent body of knowledge. He showed that attachment of the young animal to the mother is not primarily a function of the dependency for food, but rather of the bodily warmth and comfort which the mother provides.

On the other hand, similar results in the areas of personality and social psychology are difficult to find. Researchers are not satisfied with their progress and it is reportedly mentioned in the literature on both these fields that they are in state of crisis (e.g. Fiske, 1974; Zavalloni and Louis-Guerin, 1979). Also the success of psychotherapy, the most extensive field applied social science, continues to hearather contentious issue. This can be demonstrated from the fact that various approaches, which are hardly compatible on psychological grounds, follow each other more and more rapidly with no apparent sign, at least not for the outsider, of a growing convergence towards generally accepted principles.

Let me give two more concrete examples of the questionable status of psychology and personality assessment. The frustration-aggression theory was put forward by Dollard and Miller (Dollard *et al.* 1939) in the late thirties. It was based on Freud's thinking and incorporated principles from learning theory. It stipulates under certain conditions relationships between frustration drive and aggression. This idea was widely accepted among professional psychologists. A simplified form has become public knowledge in Western countries. Nowadays unemployed youngsters in Britain and The Netherlands will use their frustration as an excuse for destructive aggression. In the meantime empirical evidence has indicated that the presumed causal relationship between frustration and aggression is largely incorrect. Social psychologists now tend to see aggression in the context of social interaction as a violation of group norms (cf. De Ridder, 1982).

The second example has to do with the applicability of psychological tests. There are psychometric standards for the quality of tests which, one might expect, would lead to a certain consensus. But in a recent survey in some West-European countries considerable differences of opinion were found between individual psychologists within countries as well as between countries, especially in respect of so-called projective tests. For example, 25% of the Dutch respondents in the survey indicated that they saw little or no use for these instruments in the evaluation of therapy as against 2% in France. At the same time 7 per cent of the Dutch and 30% of the French psychologists reported that they considered projective techniques useful in more than 90% of the cases in which the success of psychotherapy with clients has to be assessed. For any outsider who thinks that there is a scientific basis to test use, such contrasts require quite a bit of explanation (cf. Poortinga *et al*, 1982).

It seems to me beyond question that projective techniques have failed almost totally to meet psychometric criteria like reliability and validity. Their continued usage by many psychologists obviously is based on different considerations. An important advantage often mentioned by those who propagate their use is that projective tests are helpful in the evaluation of factors which are unique to an individual person at a specific time. Of course, it is these kinds of factors which are not easily distinguishable from measurement error and which tend to be eliminated in psychometric analyses of validity and reliability. However, this cannot form a justification as long as no other form of empirical evidence supporting the validity of projective tests is available.

The two examples mentioned appear to justify the claim that systematic psychological knowledge in the areas mentioned is still too fallible to serve as a basis for prediction of actual behaviours. If the reason given for the continued use of projected tests is correct, this supports moreover the point that contextual factors, in this case associated with the 'uniqueness' of the individual person, preempt accurate prediction.

What has been said so far largely concerns the explanation and prediction of individual behaviours. This does not exclude the possibility that seemingly random events at the individual level may show considerable order and structure at the conglomerate level of the group. However, I would argue that the record of sociology and anthropology in the prediction of social reality is certainly not more impressive than that of psychology. If the viewpoint is correct that accuracy of prediction decreases with the number of cultural factors possibly exerting an influence, this may not be surprising.

There is a widespread tendency to treat societies as systems. In any explanatory framework the parameters controlling the system are listed far from exhaustively. In a prediction equation only the most prominent factors are taken into consideration, i.e. factors with a substantial expected effect on future events. Expected effect is usually expressed as the product of two quantities namely the importance or weight attached to an event and the probability of its actual occurrence. The combined impact of any number of factors with low weights will remain minimal unless their occurrences are interdependent. But the combined effects of high-weight low-probability factors is not negligible. If their number is large enough the probability of one or a few of these actually taking place becomes very high. Once such an unlikely event has become reality its large weight means that it will have a considerable impact on the state of affairs, although such an effect was not predicted. Nobody has expressed more forcefully the role of apparent trivialities than Pascal in his famous aphorism to the effect that today the face of the world would have looked different if the nose of Cleopatra would have been a bit shorter.

Elaborating on this point, I would like to look for a moment at the type of phenomena which determine social reality at the group level. For the present purpose these can be described as social and economic variables which affect the well-being of the members of a society. A major difficulty is that well-being is a rather subjective entity, unless we define objectivity in terms of agreement among observers. In that case variables like level of income, access to formal education and health care, nutritional status, social mobility and absence of discrimination probably can be taken as sufficiently objective indices. These are broad labels, but the need to keep the number of variables within bounds, implies that we have to look for factors which are fairly general.

In any case, it is quite certain that in few of the predictions of our Iranian colleagues the fundamentalistic Muslim movement was entered a decade ago, at least not with the appropriate weights. The consequent errors of prediction need no further comment. The sudden questioning and abandoning of prevalent social norms starting in the late sixties in Western Europe and North America was generally not foreseen. Although we feel that in retrospect we can satisfactorily understand why these changes took place the consequences apparently were not all evident. In the wake of these social changes youngsters in The Netherlands started to leave at an earlier age than before their parents' house to live on themselves (Van Leeuwen, 1971). This has been claimed to be a major factor behind the current shortage of housing, but it was unforeseen. A contemporary issue with serious implications for many societies has to do with the most desirable balance between social integration and the cultural identity of different groups living together in a single country. With attitudes stressing group identity apparently easily aroused can anyone predict the course of intergroup relationships in societies such as India or Belgium?

Several objections can be raised against the somewhat pessimistic outlook presented so far. Maybe the most plausible objection is that the limited value of many predictions in the social sciences would have been generally recognized if it were so obvious as suggested here. For a variety of reasons this is not a valid argument. It has evolved from research on decision making that human observers can show notorious shortcomings in the estimation of the probabilities of uncertain events.[3] In addition, the history of sorcery, fortune telling and superstition makes clear that a low success ratio can easily sustain existing beliefs. Furthermore, the a priori probability of certain kinds of predictions may be quite high, especially when the alternatives are not presented in an all or none fashion. A vocational guidance counsellor who states that a client has 70 per cent chance to get through university can hardly be taken to task if the clients fails. If the client is doing rather well at secondary school the statement may in fact predict nothing, beyond what was known already by this pupil and the parents and teachers.

However, there is also another side. From what has been said it follows that wrong prediction may not be so much a proof of incorrect insight as of incomplete representation of relevant factors in the theory or model on which that prediction is based. Implicit in all scientific explanation there is a so-called *ceteris paribus* condition, i.e. it is assumed that all conditions outside the frame of reference of a prediction remain constant. Unfortunately social reality encompasses a host of social variables, as well as non-social factors with an impact on society, including even the effect of scientific enquiry and prediction itself. Given the fact that we can take only limited aspects out of the total context independent of whether we pursue more holistic or more molecular variables, the most meaningful if not the only possible strategy is to disregard factors with a low probability of occurrence.

At the same time this puts into a different perspective the discrepancy between post hoc explanation, of if you like the 'understanding' of social reality, and prediction into the future. Afterwards we can incorporate in our description of what actually happened the effect of what I have indicated as low probability contextual factors.

Of course, all this raises the question what the relevance for society is of knowledge which is too incomplete for valid forecasting. Or alternatively, when is knowledge solid enough to be recommended for use in social policy making.

With the help of a simple decision making scheme (in which a decision is taken as a single-stage, binary choice) this question will be explored a bit further. The scientist has two options, namely trying to get society to act on the basis of available knowledge or, alternatively waiting until more definite expectations can be formulated and not to undertake any action. Associated with each of these two possibilities there are usually positively valued outcomes and negatively valued outcomes. The two strategies combined with the two kinds of outcome can be represented in a 2 x 2 table. A concrete example is the following. There are indications that an economic factor, namely the need for support in their own old age is an important determinant of parents' desire to have a large family (Kagitcibasi, 1982). Learning theories lead us to believe that immediate rewards are more effective in shaping behaviour than long-term rewards (Dews, 1960). So, it might be predicted that an economic gain to a couple each year before a child is born to them will lead to a decrease in population growth. Implementation of this idea actually might not result in this positive outcome. A negative outcome would be that couples profit for a number of years and thereafter still have a big family, the age of child bearing of the women being shifted. On the other hand, when no action was undertaken a positive outcome would result if the money not spent on young couples somehow would stimulate industrial growth, which in turn would diminish the economic need for children. A negative outcome of no action would be continued population growth. Thus, each of the four entries in the table can be attributed a certain expected value, or utility.

For many countries continues population growth is obviously the outcome of overriding importance and policies to bring the growth rate down might be undertaken against fairly low odds of the original prediction actually being correct. Thus, in the application of uncertain knowledge the potential costs of erroneous prediction have to be balanced against the costs of not undertaking any action at all.

The example can be extended one step further. Even though the probability of success of the proposed action may be fairly low the information on which it is based can have a high probability of being correct. In other words we may have strong empirical support for the opinion that economic factors are of real importance in family planning. This would enable us to make a prediction with a high probability of being correct, namely that any population policy which does not take into account the economic factor is almost doomed to fail. It may well be that the utility of the social sciences lies more in the discouragement of some of the courses of action which are being contemplated than in the positive recommendation of any specific action.

It can be argued that the positivistic approach implicitly followed here has insufficient scope to incorporate the explanation of behaviour and social events as the consequence of goal-directed action and self-reflection. In my view the empirical support for the predictive utility of alternative paradigms is poor. I would rather suggest that there are inherent limitations to the predictability of the phenomena we are interested in (Poortinga, 1982). This does not mean that social scientists in their role as citizens of a particular country cannot participate in goal-directed social action. It only means that we have to distinguish carefully between what we can say as scientists and what we want to say in any other role.

If there is a lesson to be learnt from the recent history of social sciences it is that explanation and prediction are far from perfect. Some of the reasons which may be intrinsic to the phenomena studied have been indicated. the should make us think twice before we engage in trying to have our knowledge applied, which is one more time than often happens.

NOTES

1. This paper was prepared while the author was a visiting professor at the Department of Psychology at he University of Allahabad.

2. It is assumed that this weight can be established unambiguously. If this is not the case the prediction equation becomes more shaky.

3. The research is of the experimental kind about which it was argued earlier that it has contributed to a more permanent body of knowledge.

REFERENCES

Catanis, A.C., *Learning*. Englewood Cliffs, J.J.: Prentice-Hall, 1979.

Corsini, R.J., *Current Psychotherapies, 2nd Ed.* Itasca, Ill.: Peacock, 1979.

De Ridder, R., De frustratie voorbij. *Psychologie*, 1982, 1, 5, 22,-30.

Dews, P.B., Free-operant behaviour under conditions of delayed reinforcement: I. CRF-type schedules. *Journal of the Experimental Analysis of Behavior*, 1960, 3, 221-234.

Dollard, J., Doob, L.W., Miller, N.E. Mowrer, O.H., and Sears, R.R., *Frustration and Aggression*. New Haven: Yale University Press, 1939.

Fiske, D.W., The limits for the conventional science of perrsonality. *Journal of Personality*, 1974, 42, 1-11.

Gibson, J.J., *The Senses Considered as perceptual Systems*. Boston: Houghton Mifflin, 1966.

Harlow, H.F. and Zimmerman, R.R., Affectional responses in the infant monkey.

Science, 1959, 130, 431-432.

Jones, E.E. and Nisbett, R.E., *The Actor and the Observer: Divergent Perceptions of the Causes of Behavior*. New York: General Learning Press, 1971.

Kagitcibasi, C., Old-age security value of children: Cross-national socioeconomic evidence. *Journal of Cross-Cultural Psychology*, 1982, 13, 29-42.

Kamin, L.J., *The Science and Politics of IQ*. Potomac Md: Lawrence Erlabaum, 1974.

Platt, J.R., Strong Inference. *Science*, 1964, 146, 347-353.

Poortinga, Y.H., Cross-culturele psychologie en minderheaden-orderzoek. *De Psycholoog*, 1982, 17, 708-720.

Poortinga, Y.H., Coetsier, P., Meuris, G., Miller, K.M., Samsonowitz, V., Seisdedos, N. and Schlegel, J., A survey of attitudes towards tests among psychologists in six Western European countries. *International Review of Applied Psychology*, 1982, 31, 7-34.

Van Leeuwen, L.Th., *Ontwikkelingsfasen van het Gezin*. Monografieen Volkstelling no 9. Den Haag: Centraal Bureau Statistiek, 1971.

Wertheimer, M., *Drei Abhandlungen zur Gestalttheorie*. Erlangen: Philosophische Akademie, 1925.

Zavalloni, M., and Louis-Guerin, C., Social Psychology at the crossroads: its encounter with cognitive psychology and the interactive perspective. *European Journal of Social Psychology*, 1979, 9, 307-321.

FOUR

Forrest B. Tyler

PERCEPTION AND SOCIAL REALITY PSYCHOSOCIAL LEAPS AND SPIRALS

People have long struggled with the question of whether the world is real; and whether if it is real, it is knowable. They have also struggled with the question of whether there is good; and, if so, whether it is attainable. I believe that our conceptions of social reality bear on both of those questions. I also believe that our conceptions of social reality in part shape and are in part shaped by our perceptions. I believe that the realities we are talking about are ongoing processes of which we are a part. Yet I also believe that neither reality nor our perceptions will remain constant. Nevertheless we can find some stability and direction for ourselves. How psychology can enlighten that undertaking and gain from it is what I would like to address.

Any point at which I might begin my presentation is somewhat arbitrary. There does not seem to be either a cleancut beginning or a clearcut end in human affairs. So I shall begin with the following statements and try to show that they are more defensible than others I might have made.

The assertion that a phenomenon, an event or an experience is real requires a leap of faith (that is a not completely supportable judgment). That does not mean that it requires or justifies the abandonment of reason (ordered experiences). The assertion that a phenomenon, an event, or an experience is good requires a judgment based on ordered experience. That does not mean that it requires or justifies the abandonment of faith or belief. Therein lies the dilemma and the salvation or destruction (at least in this life) of humans and humanity. Therein also lies the nemesis of psychology and of many fields of learning and of faith. They have all too often entrapped themselves in an effort to separate the two completely or to explain the one completely in terms of the other. To outline all of those struggles is beyond the scope of this paper. However, to sketch some of psychology's struggles with those issues may provide a useful (that is, somewhat real and good) perspective on our understanding of perception and social reality in both psychological terms and at more general levels of human understanding and discourse.

The History of Psychology and the Personal Equation

Although psychology as a discipline has been notoriously ahistorical, our understanding of perception and social reality will be severely hampered unless we include a historical perspective. However, I think that the necessary historical considerations can be highlighted by going back only some two hundred years. Specifically, historians of psychology characteristically refer to a series of events in astronomy beginning in 1796 at Greenwich Observatory as of seminal importance to psychology. Kinnebrook, the astronomer royal, discovered that his assistant, Maskelyne, deviated from him in a consistent fashion in reporting observations of star positions. He took two actions. He dismissed his assistant but he also reported the situation of other astronomers. They investigated the situation in their own observatories and by 1815 had all come to accept that they could not eliminate this "personal equation". They then concluded that they were studying human observations, not the stars (Boring, 1929). How to deny, ignore, avoid, transcend, or incorporate this conclusion in their own work has preoccupied psychologists since that time. At times, positivistic science, experimental rigor and statistical sophistication have been advocated as transcendent solutions. I will not recount the limitations of all those approaches, only their central problem, that of the role of human judgment. And to that problem Churchman, a statistician, has provided compelling arguments that there is no way of eliminate the human judgmental factor from decisions about whether a hypothesis has been confirmed or refuted by empirical findings (1948).

More recently this issue of the personal equation has been fought on other grounds. B.F. Skinner, in his book *Beyond Freedom and Dignity* (1971), argued that such terms as freedom, choice, etc. are illusory, prescientific conceptions which illserve humans individually and collectively. Rebutting that argument, Lefcourt (1973) has argued that beliefs in freedom and self-determination are indeed illusions, but so are beliefs in external control and determination. He then goes on to argue that the illusion chosen (the leap taken), freedom or determination, however, has very significant consequences for the survival and well being of the individual choosing. Further he marshalls substantial empirical evidence in support of his view (Lefcourt, 1973, 1976). The general import of that evidence is that individuals make judgments about the extent to which they do or can control situations. Those judgments, in turn, affect how the reality of situations is defined and consequently how situations impact on the people in them. For example, people who believe more strongly that they control their lives take better care of their health. People who believe that they control their lives also learn more from experiences, particularly if they judge those experiences to be subject to mastery or control through skilled performance. In effect our judgments as to the nature of the world serve to some extent to change our realities. For on the basis of those judgments we begin spirals for good or ill of exploration and verification or of withdrawal and avoidance.

Now I do not wish to suggest that simply by an act of judgment we change reality. I am not referring to such a trivial or easily refuted idea. Yet, I do wish to argue that there is validity to this idea, and that it has profound consequences for our understanding of ourselves and our world. Pursuing this point further and from two slightly different perspectives may help to make its implications clear. Specifically, the fields of sociology of knowledge and of philosophy have contributed perspectives on the nature of scientific knowledge which are relevant to the present discussion.

Karl Mannheim in his masterpiece *Ideology and Utopia* (1960) introduced and utilized a sociological approach to understanding the origins and nature of human knowledge and thereby created the field of sociology of knowledge. He was more concerned with political knowledge and arguments than with psychological ones; nevertheless, his arguments are applicable to psychology. He outlined how knowledge systems are acquired as a function shared collective experiences. He also indicated how the people who consider these systems to be reality become aware that they have just perspectives on reality, that others are possible, and that others may be preferable. Bases of such awareness and shifts may include, for example, changed ecological circumstances (as with climate changes) or confrontations with conflicting knowledge systems. Their interactions or struggles generate a sociopolitical context which serves further to shape the knowledge systems which emerge.

One confrontation of that type is of particular relevance to our current discussion. It occurred in Western Europe after the Middle Ages and gave rise to modern day science. As an artisan-based middle class emerged its members found themselves in competition with the royalty and the clergy for influence and power in shaping the nature of society and their role in it. The chief power base of the royalty and the clergy rested on their unique of special status. That is, the royalty ruled by divine right and the clergy ruled by divine right and the clergy ruled by virtue of their closer links with the deity and their special access to truth and wisdom.

In contrast the knowledge and power of artisans were based on empirically developed and verified procedures and skills which were in principle available to anyone. Thus as they contended for power they argued for rejection of the concept that anyone has special or unique access to truth. In effect they rejected not only divine revelation or dispensation as a criterion of truth and morality, but they also rejected the validity of unique individual secular experiences. They argued for building reality on evidence from procedures that anyone could use and check. They argued for a different leap of faith and they built a quite different reality.

Even today sciences, including psychology, work within a knowledge system designed to exclude the possibility of valid unique individual insights or contributions to knowledge. This point is one which increasingly requires resolution as circumstances change and we re-examine these systems. That is, our view of knowledge and reality seems to need in some way to be adapted. It needs to include a role for some uniqueness to be "variable error" or "constant error" in measurement. That is, there seem to be growing pressures to re-introduce the "personal equation" while not abandoning science entirely. Then a new spiral can begin.

Philosophers consider it their role in life to comment on the work of others and often are quite outspoken about what they consider to be the errors or shortcomings of other fields as well as wiser course of actions for those fields. For example, it was the philosopher P.W. Bridgman who was instrumental in the widespread acceptance of logical positivism as a basis for conceptualizing psychological theory and conducting psychological research. He later recanted his position (1959) and asserted that science is not solely a public enterprise, rather it is a private endeavor. Psychologists were well into a spiral of positivistic knowledge development at that point so paid less attention to his recantation. However there have been other philosophical inquiries into the nature of knowledge and values over the last twenty-five years. They have introduced a new element into their arguments, namely, appeal to psychological evidence. In that way they have made a leap to a different evidential base and begun a different kind of knowledge development spiral. For example, in 1968 Polanyi a distinguished philosopher of science at Oxford, discussed the relationship of logic to psychology in an address to the American Psychological Association. He asserted at that time that "No rules can account for the way a good idea is found for starting an inquiry, and there are no firm rules either for the verification or the refutation of the proposed solution of a problem" (p. 27). He added that in spite of this state of affairs

> Nothing is more certain in our world than the established results of science. My point is that the **absence of strict criteria** on which to base our acceptance of science merely shows that our confidence in scientific knowledge **is based on nonstrick criteria**. Science is grounded, and is firmly grounded on the kind of indefinable insights which the current view of science regards as mere psychological phenomena, incapable of producing rational inferences (p. 27).

He then utilized a perspective of perceptual analysis and appealed to data from psychological experiments on perception to make several additional points. Specifically, all knowledge contains an **indeterminant content** whenever it bears on reality. The coherence on which we accept a discovery to be true can only be **vaguely defined.** The data on which a discovery rests **are not fully identifiable**. He then demonstrated that in each of these instances, the so-called "hard criteria of science" rest inevitably on the "soft criteria" simply can not be eliminated. In short, scientific judgements rest on subjective criteria and are subject to very human limitations. Yet science does contribute important "provisional certainties". And Polanyi has, in the form of his argument, outlined for us a picture of spirals of knowledge development, outlined for us a picture of spirals of knowledge development encompassing knowledge fields and contributing to that process. That is, he has used epistemology and psychology to inform each other.

Thomas Kuhn has revolutionized much of current thinking about science and reality with his conceptions of scientific knowledge as relative to the scientific paradigms in which it exists and with his conception of scientific progress as involving discontinuous shifted from paradigm to paradigm. He is considered to be a historiographer of science. That is, in his writing he builds arguments by including historical considerations as well as philosophical ones and psychological ones (1969). He analyses the nature of reality in science at different points in history to demonstrate that scientific reality does change as our paradigm change. He also utilizes findings from psychological perception studies to argue that reality is a construction. It is derived from experientially based patterns of sensation whose influence occurs prior to perception, that is, prior to interpretation of sensory input. In short, he provides a largely parallel argument to that of Polanyi about the presence and influence of "tacit" or "soft" criteria.

Both Kuhn and Polanyi make the argument that the nature of these soft criteria is not fully subject to our inquiry. If you will, both writers denote the presence of the "personal equation" but they do not define it as it is in principle not definable. Rather they point out that our knowledge systems are subject to periodic disruptions of shifts whose nature is not totally understandable from a scientific perspective. Further, when those shifts occur they change not only the nature of scientific theories, they change reality.

The type of arguments developed and advanced by scholars such as Kuhn and Polanyi can also be utilized to scrutinize the role of values or preferences in the pursuit and nature of science and in defining reality, George McClure, a philosopher, and I (1966) developed such an argument to make the points that preferences play a role which cannot be totally eliminated in our decisions about facts and in turn facts have such a role in our decisions about preferences or values. We were not proposing that these reciprocal roles are trivial or matters of personal Machiavellianism. Nor were we proposing that facts and values are the same. It was our argument that in a very basic way factual information is necessary to the formulation of preferences or values and the nature of the information available to us shapes the form of our values. We can express preferences only among those alternatives of which we are cognizant. Conversely, the nature and range of our preferences shapes the facts that will enter into our perception of reality. If we do not or cannot distinguish differences in the desirability of alternative courses, we will not explore or acquire the information and skills essential to attaining them. Thus if the affluent and privileged members of a society can persuade the deprived and oppressed members of society that there is no preferential difference between their living situation, the deprived ones will not explore or learn what affluence is like or how to become affluent.

We did argue at that time that a common and basic procedural assumption, though it is not an "absolute value," has guided scientific enterprises. That assumption involves a committment to being guided by "procedural control" in the sense of "knowledge of the limits, assumptions, characteristics, and defects of the particular procedure one is following at the moment, and of the general systems within which one operates" (p.84). That is, in general it is considered undesirable to reduce our knowledge of what we are doing. However, Polanyi (1963) has indicated that even in the area of procedural control there are choices to be made. Specifically, he has argued that for the progress of science it is desirable and necessary that the discipline of scientific authority expressed in required adherence to dominant theoretical paradigms must be maintained. It must be maintained even to the point of rejecting contrary evidence at time. In support of his argument Polanyi cites the scientific community's rejection of his work for thirty years because it falsified parts of Einstein's theory of relativity. The justification he provides for the desirability of selective rejection of evidence is that the efforts of scientists will not be sufficiently focused to provide for major scientific advances unless there is such discipline. In short he is arguing that certain preferences of values not only guide us toward selecting facts, but that it is desirable that they do so. Of course he also argues that collections of facts do, and should, guide us in selecting certain preferences of values. Thus he argues for a form of fact-value interaction such as that which Mcclure and I asserted it inherently the case. However, we merely proposed that the situation is part of how scientists, philosophers, and ordinary people proceed and should be acknowledged and integrated into our enterprises. He has provided a particular example and used it to argue that adherence to a value position (adherence to scientific authority) can serve useful purposes. I would only add that it would seem to follow that this state of affairs can also serve negative purpose. Our value choices and our factual choices can involve us in destructive spirals as well as constructive ones.

Psychological Theory and Research

At this point I would like to turn a little more directly to the human condition as thought about and studied by psychologists, keeping in mind that the personal equation is always with us. I shall be very selective in focusing on materials that seem to me to be particularly pertinent to our topic of perception and social reality.

First let me note that humans as a species have particularly well developed characteristic of abstracting and symbolizing their experience, their reality, and themselves. Further, humans are highly malleable, they learn vastly more than other species. They also exhibit tool making and other manipulative characteristics that enable them to shape their lives and environments and record their experiences in ways that influence future generation as well as themselves. Finally, they change their date or realities in rather unique ways. That is, to digress for a moment, even physicists have noted and come to accept that the very act of measuring something changes it. However humans change their reality and themselves by measurement not only in that direct way but in other and more complex ways as well. That is, people are apparently involved in interpreting the purpose of the person measuring them and they are also interested in using the results of those measurements to change their conception of themselves and their world. Almost all humans who have taken a psychological test are aware of their reactions to being tested, of their attempts to figure out what the examiner was tying to do, of their interest in the outcome of the test and of their redefining themselves and changing their conduct as a function of the test. That is, they changed the reality themselves in at least two ways as a result of being measured; first as subjects defining themselves and their understanding of their world on the basis of the test experience and the test results.

This active and self-reflective characteristic of humans has invited considerable psychological effort to explain it away by reducing it to primitive homeostatic characteristics. However, over the past twenty-five years there have been increasingly widespread efforts to argue and marshal evidence in support of a position that these characteristics are not reducible in that fashion. Rather they must be considered in other terms. A pioneer in these efforts has been the psychologist Robert White (1959). He has been and mustered evidence to support his position that humans (and other mammals) are characterized by an effectance motivation. That is they are characterized by on active, mastery-oriented approach to their life events which produces both mastery and a sense of efficacy. He cites evidence from the exploratory, playful, and environmental manipulative characteristics of humans and mammals in their interactions with their animates as well as their inanimate environments. Although there continues to be contention about the value of conceptions of humans as active mastery-oriented creatures, there is also a growing body of research and findings in support of that position. And for the purpose of the present discussion I shall make the leap of assuming that position to be a valid factually grounded position with the weight of evidence in its favor.

Moving on then from the position of assuming that humans are active and mastery-oriented creatures, I would like to suggest that implicit in what I've been arguing is also the assertion that they are also psychosocial creatures. That is, they acquire their natures as a function of both their individual experiences and their social context. Since both of these contributing factors are quite complex I can only illustrate some of their impact and some of its consequences for forming our perceptions of ourselves and our conceptions of social reality. To do so I will cite briefly some selected psychological studies.

I have already mentioned the quite extensive and quite complex literature derived from what is usually called "basic research" on perception and the nature of reality to which Polanyi and Kuhn have referred. The preponderance of those studies are consistent with the position of those writers and of this paper. They vary in details and in conceptions as to the nature of the process involved. Nevertheless they support the view that human perception is to some extent an active integrative process which shapes and is in turn shaped by psychosocial process. Thus, perception partially defines and in turn is partially defined by social reality.

Let me also note that there have been extensive studies on the patterns of perceptual development in new born infants and young children. Those studies have included work on infant bonding, begins almost immediately with birth and that the early contact experiences of an infant make a difference in its perception of the nature of the world and in its general development (Bowlby, 1969, 1980).

Let me move on to look at the more complex picture that we encounter in older children, adolescents and adult when we study their ways of interacting with their world and their views of themselves and of their world. In doing so I want to cite some example which illustrate the pattern I have been describing. That is, these studies illustrate how individual choose (make a leap of faith) particular types of perception, and then how those choice lead them to build on that perceptual view in a fashion that resembles a spiral.

For example, a doctoral thesis was recently conducted by O.P. Shrivastava (1981) under the directorship of Dr. R.K. Naidu. The objective of the study was to explore the differences in characteristics among handicapped children who handle their life situations well and those who do not. Two particularly striking difference occur between those groups. On measures of stress and stress resistance those who handle their situation better reported less stress. They also reported using relatively more task oriented and positive strategies rather than defensive ones for handling stress. Further, the two groups reported different patterns of attribution to cause of their suffering and to support-giving agents providing them with resources to cope with their life situations. Those handling their handicaps poorly listed members of their family as the primary cause of their handicaps and themselves as their chief resource. They ranked their family third as a resource. Those handling their handicaps well list God and others belonging to society as the primary cause of their handicaps but also list God as the primary source of their strength to handle their life situations. The issue here is not the accuracy of their attributions which is, at least to a considerable extent, not determinable. The point is that individuals who have a reciprocally supportive conception (or perception) of the source of their problems and their solutions and who have more positive approaches to coping with their problems have put together a basis for a more constructive and efficacious approach to defining and coping with their lives.

Let me cite another study which may serve to illustrate another facet of this pattern of attribution or leap of faith and construction of spirals of individual-world interaction. My colleagues and I conducted a study of over 250 high school students. We were investigating the factors which influence how well those students were integrating their lives and how they would respond to a counselling program. The central findings for that study do support the hypothesis that students who are more actively planful and mastery oriented and who have a stronger sense that they are responsible for their own lives are judged by their counselors and teachers to be handling their own lives more meaningfully and effectively (Tyler and pargament, 1981). However, what I want to describe are some findings that are somewhat tangential to that central purpose. Specifically, I want to call attention to the characteristic different in the ways in which adolescents construct their senses of responsibility for their lives (Tyler, Gatz, and keenan, 1979). One of the measures used in that study is a widely used measure of locus of control (Rotter, 1966). That scale is designed to measure the extent to which individuals consider the events in their lives to be a function of their own actions (internal control) or of actions and factors external to them (external control). We analyzed that scale further and determined that it is more accurate to say that it measures the extent to which persons consider themselves to be active (creating opportunities and outcomes), passive agents (actively responding to opportunities but not creating them) or victims (unable to influence events in any fashion). It was our basic hypothesis that males and females have been socialized differently in relation to their roles in life and will reflect those differences in their patterns of attribution. Our analysis of the response patterns of these students did yield results consistent with our expectations. Specifically, "we found that males asserted strong internal control over task areas of their lives; they did not over their personal lives or over the system (institutional forces) generally. Females seemed to reflect a view of the world as made up of situations in which, once chance or fate has lined things up, they can behave internally and create their desired outcomes. Further, they seemed to believe that in the long run, chance factors will even things out so that they will have their share of opportunities" (p. 33, 1979).

In brief, at an overall level these girls did not attribute more influence to external factors then the boys did, yet they did construct a distinctively different conception of the nature of events and of their role in their own lives. Further these differences seem consistent with characteristic differences in the socialization of boys and girls in the American culture. Finally, it seems reasonable to suggest that once these perceptual differences have been formulated they serve to undergird distinctively different spirals of psychosocial functioning and development. However, we did not in that project study that possibility. There are, however other studies which support the inference that once attribution patterns are formed they do influence the spiraling patterns of interaction and senses of reality that that that that individuals develop (Lefcourt, 1976).

Our different Social Realities

It is time to turn our attention to some of the implications of the arguments and evidence which have been presented thus far. In short, how do these points enlighten our understanding of our social realities. I have sought to make the point that each of us is involved in shaping and being shaped by the events in our lives. We are to some extent mastery-oriented symbolizing creatures. We selectively organize perceptions out of the "blooming buzzing confusion" of events and do so in part as a function of experiences which we cannot symbolize. Those experiences are imbedded in us at a point prior to symbolization. Yet as we do formulate symbolized conceptions of our internal and external reality they in turn shape our actions and interpretations of subsequent events. Thus it is meaningful to characterize our patterns of interactions as consisting of leaps of faith and spirals of reality construction. I have also suggested that at a more general or institutional level it is possible to discern comparable patterns of interaction in the adoption, development, and changing of knowledge system and belief system. For example, I cited the reciprocal interactions between psychologists and philosophers in which each informs and is informed by other.

I now want to suggest that as scholars we are being confronted more frequently with evidence of the ubiquitous presence of such leaps of faith and spirals of reality construction. They characterize our ways of defining events, reality, and ourselves. It is becoming increasingly difficult to justify our current position that we can avoid making such leaps.

For example, in the realm of individual psychological functioning there have been numerous attempts to identify or establish the essence of human nature and human well being former. At least one aspect of our humanity that has been the focus of considerable attention is our sexuality. In fact Sigmund Freud made the leap to posit that our psychosexuality is indeed the core of our being. He went on to build on that premise a theory of pathology, therapy, and personality. More recently efforts have been made to extend that model to other cultures. Kakar, an Indian psychoanalyst has examined the various modern and traditional psychologically relevant healing practices in India (1983). He has reported on those approaches, noted the frequent involvement of sexual issues in the problems dealt with, and quite often reinterpreted the nature of those problems and treatments in psychoanalytic terms. He directly asserts his belief in a universal human nature and his belief in its Freudian character.

What I wish to assert is that the assumption of a universal human nature, sexual or otherwise, seems quite incompatible with the material I have been presenting. It seems to me to be a more defensible leap of faith to assert that there are a multitude of human natures, including psychosexual natures. In short, psychosexual functioning, pathology, and well being are so much an integral part of our overall psychosocial development that they are more likely to have different, though possibly overlapping, realities. Thus it seems quite unlikely that the psychosexual reality of an Orissan tribal couple and an upper class Viennese couple of the early 1900's are in any profoundly psychological sense the same reality.

Another type of illustration of the notion that people live in different psychosocial realities can be found in psychological studies from World War II. That war was quite unique in its scope and in the fashion in which it brought individuals with quite different cultural histories together under common combat stress considerations. To some extent those situations provided a natural laboratory for studying the role psychosocial factors play in human coping with severe stress, disintegration under that stress, and recovery from that disintegration. The India-Burma theatre provided some particularly relevant findings in the contrasts between British and Indian soldiers in their ways of coping with that situation. They shared the same battlefields and were subjected to the same psychiatric conceptions, analyses, and treatments. The Indian soldiers were less troubled than the British by hand to hand fighting ands gorilla warfare, and expressed less guilt about killing the enemy. They, however, were more distressed than the British at the possibility of losing face, that is prestige and self-esteem, within their unit by for example, showing signs of anxiety or fear.

The dysfunctional reactions of both groups to the Combat situation were consistent with their world views. British soldiers did talk about their anxieties and in that way helped themselves and each other to cope with them. However, consistent with what was acceptable in their culture they also exhibited more "anxiety disorders". In contrast the Indian soldiers exhibited more "hysterical disorders". That is, they had fits or convulsions or developed functional paralyses, loss of voice, or distorted postural symptoms such as a wry or twisted neck. These symptom patterns were reported to be similar to the public displays of Indian ascetics. They seemed to choose dysfunctional responses which were culturally acceptable.

The patterns of breakdown and recovery were also different for these two groups. The British suffered more breakdowns under the anticipatory anxiety of waiting for battle; the Indians under post battle conditions. The Indians may well have endured more stress (from the point of view of an outside observer) before they broke down. They also were less likely to recover ands took longer to do so presumably because they had suffered a more severe lose of status and self-esteem (Mandelbaum, 1954).

What are we to make of these findings? I would like to suggest first that we make the leap and consider that these Indian and British soldiers were dealing with somewhat different internal and external realities. Let us then build our understanding on that postulation. Let me assert that there is more than one way of being human and of defining reality. Further those different patterns provide alternatives which have characteristic strengths and limitation. Let us consider that life is not and cannot be an errorless enterprise. No matter how complete our anticipation and preparation we cannot anticipate totally nor prepare fully for what we all encounter. We can more profitably think of ourselves as somewhat open systems, that is as somewhat self-correcting and selfimproving or self-destroying living beings. We live nested in social and non-social contexts which are themselves changing and shaping both themselves and us. Those contexts are also being changed and shaped by us individually and collectively. We can do make leaps of faith and then construct spirals of self, world, and interactive development. They serve us well at times and guide our collapse at others. I would suggest that such a characterization is perhaps the most apt that we can provide for describing these soldiers in their finer moments as well as in their breakdowns and recoveries. The Indian soldiers and the British soldiers lived in somewhat different realities and reflected those differences in their distinctive ways of competing with what might seem to an outsider to be a common situation

Perhaps another and briefer illustration will serve to make these points clearer. There has been a recent and widespread interest in the potential role of women as of equal significance individually and socially to that of men. There has also been interest in the role of women as important in its own right, not just in relation to the role of men. This view is in sharp contrast to numerous historical and cultural traditions which have been the lives and the role of women as meaningful only in relation to men. One country which has been particularly caught up in struggles between its historical conception of itself and its efforts to mold a more enlightened future is Israel. Its people have also been quite self-consciously concerned with their own identity and desires for realisation of better individual and collective lives for their people. That orientation plus a relatively high degree of psychological-mindedness has stimulated a wealth of psychological studies. In one of those studies Datan (1970) investigated the ease and constructiveness with which Isreali women coped with menopause. She found that very traditional women and very liberated women handled menopause well. However, those women who were transition between traditional and liberated roles had significantly more difficulty. It would seem that traditional and liberated realities served reasonably well though in possibly quite different ways as quides for coping with this major life change. The uncertain reality of those women who were not clearly committed to either role served them much less well when they were faced with the external and internal pressures associated with menopause. That is not to say that there is neither a time nor a place for examination of one's faith and for choosing others on which to build. But it is to say that both examination of one's faiths and reliance on them for constructing patterns of living have their uses, their limitations, and their appropriate times.

I do not wish to overlook or ignore the issues arising from the relationships among different collective realities such as the knowledge-belief systems which we call academic disciplines and those we call the ethos of nations or cultures. As I noted earlier, fields of inquiry such as philosophy and psychology have shown some inclination to utilize their different leaps of faith and resulting constructions to inform and enlighten each other. At a level of national or cultural exchanges it was found in the studies I mentioned earlier that British and Indian Soldiers could also enhances each other range and patterns of coping with their somewhat common situation. These examples hardly do more than illustrate the broader point I wish to make, but let me pass on to it. At the microcosmic level of individuals, families, and small groups, as well as at the macrocosmic level of disciplines, religions, cultures, and nation-states the issues of perception and social reality are compellingly important. And they are remarkably similar. It seems equally untenable to believe that we live in totally different worlds and to believe that we all live in the same world.

Rather the arguments and evidence I have advanced seem more supportive of a leap of faith to the belief that there are convergent, divergent, and conflicting areas of experience and reality between and two of us. Be we individuals, families, communities, or cultures we have some comparable experiences, some unique experiences, and some conflicting experiences. We, individually and collectively, inform ourselves and each other of the limitations as well as the strengths inherent in our respective realities. We can build on our commonalities, honour our differences, and contain our conflicts in less destructive and more mutually beneficial ways than is now often the case. It is, of course, my conviction and my hope that psychological approaches and perspectives have and will contribute to that enterprise and have and will be enriched by it.

EPILOGUE

I wish to add as a final comment, I do not believe we will ever reach a utopia or Nirvana in the human condition. Each new generation begins by constructing its own new realities in its own new context. As I noted earlier, our individual and collective existences seem better described and understood as somewhat open systems. To some extent we create them and enhance them as well as limiting them and destroying them. I can hope for and work toward the possibility that future generations will struggle with and enrich themselves from similar as well as different concerns. I hope they can make leaps of faith and construct their realities under conditions of less threat of mass destruction. I hope they live in conditions of less mass vulnerability to potentially controllable factors such as floods, wars, famines, and social injustices. I'm sure that whatever their situation roles such as that of active agentry, passive agentry, and victimization will have their place in some form or other. So will the issues of belief and doubt. I do not know whether the Hindu conception of a universe which exhibits a continuing cycle of creation and dissolution has validity. But I do think that a conception of the lives of successive generations as characterized by creation, development, and dissolution does have validity. That's a leap of faith I can make and on which I can build.

NOTE

This paper was completed when the author was the visiting professor in the Department of Psychology, University of allahabad.

REFERENCES

Boring, E.G.,*A history of experimental psychology*, New York: Appleton-Century, 1929

Bowlby, J., *Attachment*, New York: Basic Books, 1969.

Bowlby, J.,*Loss, sadness and depression*, New York: Basic Books, 1980.

Bridgman, P.W.,*The way things are*, New York Viking Press, 1959.

Datan, N.; Maoz, B. Antonovosky, A., and Wiisenbeek, H., Climacterium in three culture contexts. *Tropical and Geographical medicine*, 1970, 22, 77-86.

Kakar, S.,*Shamans, Mystics and doctors*, Delhi: the Oxford University Press, 1933.

Kuhn, T.S., *The structure of scientific revolutions* (second edition, revised and enlarged) Chicago: The University of Chicago Press, 1969.

Lefcourt, H.M., *Locus of control*, New York: Wiley, 1976.

Mandelbaum, D.G. Psychiatry in military society I.,*Human Organization*, 1954, 13, No. 3.

Mannheim, K.*Ideology and Utopia*, London: Routledge and Kegan Paul, 1960.

McClure, G. and Tyler, G.B. Policy decisions in science: Psychological considerations and implications for psychology, *The Journal of General Psychology*, 1966. 77, 69-86.

Polanyi, M., The potential theory of adsorption, *Science*, 1963, 141, 1010-1013.

Polanyi, M., Logic and Psychology, *American Psychologist*, 1968, 23, 27-43.

Rotter, J., Generalized expectancies for internal versus external control of reinforcement, *Psychological Monographs*, 1966, No. 609.

Shrivastava, O.P., *Stresses and coping mechanisms of physically handicapped children*, Unpublished doctoral dissertation, University of Allahabad, 1981.

Skinner, B.F.,*Beyond freedom and dignity*, New York: Alfred A. Knopf, 1971.

Tyler, F.B., Gatz, M. and Keenan, K., A constructivist analysis of the Rotter I-E scale, *Journal of Personality*, 1979, 47, 11-35.

Tyler, F.B. and Pargament, K.I., Racial and personal factors and the complexities of competence-oriented changes in a high school group counseling program, *American Journal of Community Psychology*, 1981, 9, 697-714.

White, R.W. Motivation reconsidered: The concept of competence, *Psychological Review*, 1959, 66, 297-333.

FIVE

Janak Pandey

CONSTRUCTION OF SOCIAL REALITY IN SOCIAL PSYCHOLOGY

The current state of social psychology has been the subject of a great deal of recent debate. The philosophical assumptions, nature of man, methodology, theory construction, relevance and applications of research in social psychology have been extensively examined particularly in the last two decades (Lana, 1969, Harre & Secord, 1972, Israel & Tajfel, 1972). Kurt Lewin, one of the foremost founding fathers of the contemporary social psychology strongly believed and integrated his theoretical thinking and research so as to support his belief that only scientific research provides reliable guidelines to effective social action. In one of his most well-known statements, Lewin suggests that "close cooperation between theoretical and applied psychology can be accomplished...if the theorist does not look toward applied problems, with highbrow aversion or with a fear of social problems, and if the applied psychologist realizes that there is nothing as practical as a good theory" (Lewin, 1951, p. 169). How far, social psychology has been able to achieve the objective envisaged by Kurt Lewin, was recently evaluated in a self-confession by a group of distinguished social psychologists closely connected with the Lewinian tradition in a volume entitled *Retrospection on social psychology* edited by Leon Festinger (1980). Leon Festinger (1980) as a concluding remark recalls a scence from the movie *The Horse's*

Mouth to describe the present state of social psychology. I reproduce Festinger's memory of the movie:

"The main character, a rather self-willed and eccentric artist, has just finished painting a mural, unauthorized, on the wall of an apartment whose owners are away on vacation. In the process he has pawned furniture, fixtures-everything Pawnable from the apartment - to pay for his oils, brushes, and models, scrupulously putting every pawn ticket in a jar. He is now about to leave. The apartment is a chaotic mess, but he has finished the mural, which is later to be considered a masterpiece, and says: "It is not exactly what I had in mind".

Leon Festinger, a key figure in making of social psychology confesses unsatisfactory state of affairs of this discipline. The social psychological theories as theories have neglected the social nature of man. Serge Moscovici (1972) asks a pertinent question: "What is social in social psychology"? As a matter of fact, social psychologists have not succeeded in creating a language, a model and a definition of problems which would genuinely correspond to social reality. The present paper is aimed to discuss some pertinent issues responsible for inadequacy in social psychological knowledge in understanding social reality and to consider some new alternative paradigm to overcome the present difficulties in social-psychological enquiry.

The assumption of empirical evaluation

Over the past forty years, the social sciences in general, and social psychology in particular, have become increasingly committed a positivist epistemological base. Perhaps, the chief assumption underlying contemporary research in social psychology is that general theoretical statements are subject to empirical evaluation. It has been frequently asserted that social psychology "....seeks to understand the factors responsible for stable relationship between events" (Jones and Gerard, 1967). Traditionally, social psychologists attempt to discover causal relationships so that they can establish basic principles that will explain the phenomena of social psychology. However, in recent years, in contrast to the positivist paradigm, there is re-emergence of concern with the extent to which knowledge in general, and social knowledge in particular, is anchored within the social millieu. The concern with the problematic character of empirical verification has been termed a"socio-rationalist" approach. Unlike, the traditional empiricist, the emphasis is not on fundamental theoretical principles but on the highly volunerable products of particular socio-historical circumstances. When the "reality" is socially constructed, and conceptions or theories of behaviour depend on social influence, then the critical assumption an "objectively based knowledge" is thrown into question. A large number of investigators have contributed to this emerging perspective. For examples, Becker's (1963) work on deviance attempted to show, for one, how the concept of deviance is socially generated and operates to the disadvantage of certain segments of society and for the benefit of others. "Deviance" is not so much an empirical reality. According to Becker, it is a label shared by a certain sector of society to sustain its way of life. In the same way, there are "conventional crimes" (Becker, 1968), that is, crimes within the "favored" sector of the culture (e.g. invasion of income tax, profiting through disadvantaging another) which are regarded as normal and appropriate. The classic works of Marx and Mannheium have demonstrated the dependence of various bodies of "established knowledge" on particular socio-cultural circumstances.

Although social psychologists within the experimental tradition have functioned in relative independence of most of these concerns, certain orientations within the field are quite compatible with these developments. The investigation of social norms (Sherif, 1935; Newcomb, 1943) has long placed an emphasis on the processes of social agreement necessary for the generation and sustenance of pattern behaviour. Similarly, social norms are often Viewed as arbitrary (e.g. agreement on "autokinetic" movement) and subject to gross transhistorical fluctuation (Pepitone, 1976). Festinger's (1954) early concern with the dependency of opinion on "social reality", and the manner in which social comparison generates judgements about self and others is compatible with the socio-rationalist perspective. The concept of "normative social influence" (Jones & Gerard, 1967) is similarly consistent with the socio-rationalist position. It supports the assumption that interpretation of the world is often reliant on the opinions of others. In general however social psychologists have lacked in their efforts of a through-going in construction of reality

The experimental approach distorts reality

The experimental paradigm which became a major empirical tool for the development of social psychology has been challenged for its utility in construction and understanding of social reality. Harre' and Secord (1972) have convincingly argued that the experimental set-up destroys the possibility of the study of the very features that are essential to social behaviour in its natural setting. Harre' (1980) comments "When the physical bearer of the psychological entity is tudied in isolation from that structure it ceases to be psychologically relevant" (P.28). The critics of experimental social psychology further argue that experiment is the wrong method for making empirical study of psychological process and products. Even the correlational method of social psychological enquiry has been under attack. The correlational method, according to Harre' (1980) is sloppy investigations using large samples and statistical operations to yield correlative factors. He comments that this is a method of agriculture and not of social behaviour. I would like to argue that adopting a particular method for all types of social behaviour has particularly created problems for social psychology, In recent years various innovative methods have been developed with genuine desire for a radical change in methodology. For example, Harre' (1980) suggests to return to single case studies and to use extensive and intensive designs. The natural scientists like anatomists use these designs to explore particular cases. Both people and social episodes can be subjected to such kind of treatment. Campbell's (1975) method of experimenting society is unique for constructing social reality of even complex social movements and socio-economic change processes.

Towards a scientific revolution

The preceding discussion suggests that conventional social psychology has been criticized on a wide range of issues. At the same time, in recent past, new approaches, paradigms and directions have been provided to reconstruct the social psychology. We plan to briefly review these newly emerging possibilities of reconstruction.

The historical thesis

Since 1973 with the publication of his paper entitled "Social

Psychology as History", Gergen has provided a historical perspective and exciting line of inquiry. Gergen (1973) in his historical thesis clearly suggests that the study of social psychology is basically a historical undertaking. According to his as social psychologists, we are essentially engaged in a systematic account of contemporary affairs. Thus, by nature social psychology is different from natural sciences. The historical thesis suggests that psychology and social psychology in particular is the study of contemporary social history. Gargen qualifies his thesis by suggesting that some social phenomena are historically durable and resistant to influence, while some other phenomena are less durable. The less durable phenomena are affected by the historical context and changes more. Gergen maintains that social psychological research is primarily the systematic study of contemporary history.

The dialectical thesis

In recent years, dialectical emphasis has been particularly been put in the study of developmental psychology (Riegl, 1976). However, Riegel's idea apply more broadly to all branches of the discipline. The dialectical psychology is concerned with "the study of actions and changes" (Riegel, 1976, p. 696). Leon Rappoport (1974) has argued that the Marxist idea of Praxis may be understood in terms of psychological constructs, and such understanding can yield **tangible, concrete** changes in psychological theory and research. In the context of psychology "The concept of Praxis in marxism refers to the transforming the world as well as aiding his own self - development" (Janousek, 1972). The dialectical approach aims to study the conflict and contradiction rather than equilibrium or stability . The objective is to search those contradictions that create individual, cultural growth and development. A dialectical perspective advocates that we grow through a process which consists of a series of oppositions. Rychlak (1968) maintains that our status at any one time is the synthesis of previous theses and antitheses. Ching (1982) from the chinese Institute of Psychology, has described that "the major task which Chinese Psychologists have faced was to emancipate it from bourgeois ideological influence and to make the science capable of service to China's socialist construction". He argues that mind is a reflection of social environment in which one lives. He further adds that "Consciousness is the mental reflection of objective reality, knowledge is acquired through the senses and enriched through practice."

The Thesis of Interdependence

Developing upon the earlier formulation found in the symbolic interactionist approaches (e.g. Blumer, 1966, Mead, 1934), Pepitone (1976) questions the adequacy of purely individual psychology that ignores the normative aspects of behaviour. Pepitone (1976) argues that "the causes of behaviour cannot be clearly and validly specified unless one defines the contours of the system or unity in which the causal progress operate" (p. 642). A purely individual psychology can not explain a large portion of behaviour studied by social psychologists. Therefore, there is a need for "a reorientation in both theory and methodology" (p. 652) so that collective, and interdependent (and normative) determinants of most behaviour can be more adequately represented in psychology.

The present aim is not to develop these three theses in detail. Rather goal is to suggest that these developments direct our attention to various shortcomings and necessary modification of our existing ways of thinking, and theorizing in social psychology.

Scientific Revolution

All those who feel concerned about the limitations of social psychology, argue that we must change the existing model of our science. Sampson (1978) comments "It is not enough .....simply to change concepts when the total array of concepts, methods, and rules for validating our work derives from an approach to science that represents and affirms a partial value perspective" (p.1332). To understand the path of scientific revolution in social psychological enquiry it is essential that we consider the natural science model (the existing dominating model of enquiry) and and the new conception about the model of science.

The natural science model - Paradigm I

According to the value orientation of the naturalistic conception of science (Paradigm I) facts and truths appear in abstract, general and universal forms, scientific knowledge and truth are considered independent of any particular society or historical period. This classic view of natural sciences has dominated social psychology. The epistemological basis of Paradigm I science suggests that universal truths are independent of time and place. Paradigm I disregards sociohistorical standpoint. The experimental method as typically employed in social psychology exemplifies Paradigm I science. Field and observation methods, however, are also based on a Paradigm I conception of proper science.

The historical model of science-paradigm II

The historical model of science (paradigm II) construes that facts and truth emerge within "specific places and times". Mannheim (1936) argues that sociohistorical standpoint on knowledge is not considered a source of error, but as an element that is intrinsic to all knowledge. The ethos of the society is mirrored in the thought forms of even scientific knowledge. As Sampson (1978) puts it: "To refer to a paradigm as historical in this sense is to recognize its embededness in a particular culture and history" (p. 1334).

Although, it may be generally difficult choice to opt for one of the paradigms, but for social psychology, Paradigm II also seems to have a strong case. Even Kuhn (1962) who recognizes the dominance of the epistemological view point (Paradigm I), sees that "it no longer function effectively". Once a paradigm gets socialized into their theory of knowledge, it does not easily relinquish its dominance, even if there is growing recognition of its failure.

Scientific paradigms actually represent and reaffirms a particular cultural ideology and value orientation (Sampson, 1978). For example, Paradigm I arose in a particular cultural context and value matrix: Puritan protestantism, individualism, male dominance, selective equality, private property, and capitalism. Paradigm I science not only found a supportive context for its own growth put helped in advances of knowledge that served the emerging society. Gradually, Paradigm I has acquired a kind of functional autonomy and therefore, it appears detached from its value origins. But, it continues to support the status quo in social psychology, including particular set of values. As Ratner (1973) has suggested, a paradigm that argues that sciences studies whatever is an immutable reality (paradigm I) can be readily reversed so that whatever science discovers "is *ipso facto* external and immutable reality" (p. 36). Buss (1975) has also argued that inadevrtantly traditional experimental social psychology has failed in studying the social basis of psychological theories.

Paradigm Shifts

The above discussion implicates that to reflect and affirm a wider range of human values and to offer a fundamentally more complete perspective on human social behaviour, social psychology must undergo a paradigm shift. Franz Samelson (1976) has provided some clue regarding the possibilities of a paradign shift. He has suggested how the background of psychologists, including their religious orientations, influenced their theories of human nature. For example, Samelson (1976) argues that when the psychological establishment was white, male, protestant in background, inherent racial and ethnic inferiority in intelligence was demonstrated. However, when this discipline attracted more ethnics, the field began to shift toward a concern with why majority were prejudiced. It is well known that socio-historical factors play an important role in paradigm choice and use. The actual paradigm shift will occur partly as a function of the mind of people are recruited in to social psychology. Samelson's contention gets support of the psychologists from developing countries. The social psychological theories of development and change under framework of paradigm I are under challenge and doubt. This has particularly happened when psychologists of the developing counties have started recognizing the role of socio-historical, economic, political, and cultural context (paradigm II) (Ching, 1982; Salazar,1982; Sinha, D., 1982, J.B.P.,1982). It seems that Paradigm II as envisaged, has a fertile social context in the developing countries for its revolutionary growth. As Sampson (1978) argues "If a cultural shift towards collectivism occurs, then we might very well see the dominance of a paradigm II social psychology.

REFERENCES

Becker, H.S., *Outsiders: Studies in the sociology of deviance* New York: Free Press, 1963,

Blumer, H., Sociological implications of the thought of George Herbert Mead. *American Journal of Sociology*, 1966, 71, 535-544.

Buss, A.R. The merging field of the sociology of psychological knowledge. *American Psychologist* 1975, 30. 988-1002.

Ching, C.C., *Psychology and the four modernization in China*. IUPS Conference on Impact of psychology on the third world development, Edinburgh, Scotland, July 24-25, 1982

Festinger, L., A theory of social comparison processes. *Human relations*, 1954, 7, 117-140.

Festingle, L., Looking backward. In L. Festinger (Ed.), *Retrospections on social psychology*. London and New York: Oxford University Press, 1980.

Gergen, K.J., Social psychology, science and history. *Personality and social Psychology Bulletin*, 1976. 2, 373-383.

Gergen, K.J.,*Towards transformation in social knowledge*. Springer - Verlag: New York, Inc., 1982.

Harre', R., Making social psychology scientific. In R. Gilmour and s. Duck (Eds.), *The development of social psychology*, New York: Academic Press, 1980.

Harre', R. and Secord, P.F. *The explanation of social behaviour* Oxford: Blackwell, 1972

Israel, J. and Tajfel, H. (Eds.), *The context of social psychology : A critical assessment*. New York : Academic Press, 1972.

Janousek, G., On the Marxian concept of praxis. In J. Israel, and H. Tajfel (Eds.), *The context of social psychology: A critical Assessment*, New York; Academic Press, 1972.

Jones, E.E., and Gerard. H.B., *Foundations of social psychology*. New York: Wiley, 1967.

Kuhn, T.S., *The structure of scientific revolutions*, Chicago: University of Chicago Press, 1962.

Lewin, K., *Field theory and social science*, New York: Harper, 1951.

Mannheim, K., *Ideology and Utopia*, New York : Harvest Books, 1936.

Mead, G.H .,*Mind, self and society from the standpoint of a social behaviorist*, Chicago, III.: University of Chicago Press, 1934.

Moscovici, S. Society and theory in social psychology. In J. Israel and H. Tajfel (Eds.), *The context of social psychology:A critical assessment,* New York: Academic press, 1972.

Pepitone, A., Toward a normative and comparative biocultural social psychology, *Journal of personality and social psychology*, 1976,34, 641-653

Rappaport, Leon, on Praxis and Quasi-rationality, *The Conference on Dialectical operations, and method*, University of Rochester, May, 1974.

Rather, J.,, Introduction to John Dewey's philosophy. In R. Handy and E.C. Hardwood (Eds.), *Useful procedures of inquiry*, great Barrington, Mass: Behavioural Research Council, 1973

Riegel,K.F., The dialectics of human development , *American Psychologist,* 1976, 31, 689-700.

Rychalak, J.F., *A philosophy of science for personality theory*. Boston, Mass: Houghton-Mifflin, 1968.

Salazar, J.M.*Psychological technology and its use in Venezuelan politics*. IUPS Conference on Impact of Psychology on the third world development, Edinburgh, Scotland, July 24-25, 1982.

Samelson, F., *From 'race-psychology' to 'studies in prejudice', Some observations on the thematic reversals in social psychology*, paper presented at the Cheiran society, Smithsonian Institution Washington, D.C. 1976.

Sampson, E.E.,Scientific paradigms and social values wanted - A Scientific revolution, *Journal of Personality and social Psychology* 1978, 36, 11, 1132-1143.

Sinha, D., *Cross-cultural Psychology: A View from the third world.* Presidential address to the VI International Congress of IACCP, Aberdeen, (Scotland), July 19-23, 1982b.

Sinha, J.B.P., *The impact of psychology on the third world development.* IUPS Conference, Edinburgh, Scotland, July 24 - 25, 1982.

SIX

Sibesh Bhattacharya

HISTORICAL REALITY SOME CONCEPTUAL AND METHODOLOGICAL COMPONENTS

We think it ought to be stated right at the beginning that our approach to the question of historical reality in this paper has been the approach of a working student of history, an approach born out of the practical considerations of the problems and difficulties faced in pursuing the discipline of history. Our approach therefore is likely to be found lacking in the extremely fine logical distinctions and the razor sharp conceptual precisions usually associated with philosophical arguments. The present paper does not have any philosophical pretension whatever; its sole ambition is to outline the way a practioner of history tries to come to terms with historical reality.

We think it also ought to be stated that we are not offering this explanation merely apologetically. Perhaps through this explanation we are trying to make a statement. The nature of historical reality has been a subject of much philosophical discussion. As a matter of fact this has been an area where the voice of the philosopher has been more dominant than that of the historian. Generally the lot of the historian has been to be treated as the humble student to be told by the philosopher teacher as to what he should try to do. Here is a typical example: 'Before history may raise its head in the company of the disciplines **certified by philosophy** as capable of warranting responsible claims to knowledge, it must be demonstrated that it is capable of satisfying the criteria of reference, factuality, truth, and objectivity **that philosophy establishes**. (Leon J. Goldstein, *Historical Knowing*, University of Texas Press, 1976, p. XI emphasis added). It is true that all historians have not been all that humble before the pontifications of philosophers. Elton, for example, doubts whether philosophical considerations of history as a discipline is of any value, if not a positive impediment, to historians. '...a philosophic concern with such problems as the reality of historical knowledge or the nature of historical thought only hinders the practice of history'. 'I do not mean to deny that there are some sensible books on these subjects, ... Every new number of **History and Theory** is liable to contain yet another article struggling to give history a philosophic basis, and some of them are interesting. But they do not, I fear, advance the writing of history'. (G.R. Elton, *The Practice of History*, Sydney University Press, 1967, p. VII cf. J.H. Plumb, *The Death of the Past*, London 1969, p. 104.) Compare the following statement regarding philosophy of science: '... the one thing working scientists are not going to do is to change their ways of thinking, in doing science, *ex more philosophico*, because they have Popper and Feyerabend pontificating at them like eighteenth-century divines'. (Margaret Masterman, 'The Nature of a Paradigm' in *Criticism and the Growth of Knowledge*, ed. Imre Lakatos and Alan Musgrave, Cambridge, 1970, p. 60). We need not go to the length of Elton and dismiss the value of philosophical investigations into the nature of history but we do desire to emphasise that the historian's view of historical reality is as important and as valid as the philosopher's view of historical reality. After all history as a discipline is the creation of historians and the nature of the discipline of history will continue to be primarily determined by the concerns, assumptions and techniques of historians despite the contemplations of philosophers and their indirect influences.

The following statement of Topolski in a general way sums up our point of view on the matter:

"The controversy about history continues.....

What should be the role of the practicing, professional historian in the controversy about history as a discipline? He can neither ignore it nor devote all his time to it. He can, however, define his own position in the debate and then exemplify it through his work. In this way he can defend his position while at the same time doing his job and building up the substantive body of knowledge on which history depends." (Jerzy Topolski, *Methodology of History*, Warsaw 1976, pp. 1-2).

It will not serve much useful purpose to attempt giving a definition of history; the task may be left to philosophers who have a natural propensity to do such jobs and who immensely enjoy doing them. Even though historians ordinarily do not care to give precise and full definition of the discipline they are engaged in they have a pretty certain idea about its subject-matter. All historians agree that the subject-matter of history is human past. Past has a finite finished quality about it, it is the very antithesis of flux; or if objection is raised against this expression, it can be restated as 'flux frozen'. This way the subject-matter of history gives its students certain advantages that are denied to those who endeavour to grapple with objects which are changing. The fixity of the character of past makes it a subject especially worth pursuing because the possibility of comprehending it is not negated right at the beginning by any inherent instability in the character of the subject itself.

Working historians do not doubt even for a moment the reality of past or to be more precise the past with which human beings had been having interaction, if they had any, they would not be writing more and more history despite being told to desist from the unprofitable labour by acute thinkers like Descartes and many others. "History, expelled from the body of knowledge proper by Descartes in part I of the *Discourse*, is still regarded with suspicion by his successors today". (W.H. Walsh, *An Introduction to Philosophy of History* London 1977, p. 12). It is also clear from the fact that an ever increasing number of historians are found pursuing their discipline that there must be some implicit faith or assumption that the reality they deal with is knowable to impel them in their works.

It is generally accepted that historical knowledge can be obtained only through rigorous painstaking research. The objective of this research is to uncover the shape of past and it involves searching out the 'sources', examining their dependability and making them yield faithful informations. Historical research thus needs at every stage industry, dedication and patience and above all a constant alertness and vigil. A historian has to keep his eyes and ears ever open. All these point to another important assumption made by historians: historical reality has an external independent existence of its own. In other words, human past, which is the subject-matter of history, in the view of working historians, has an objective basis outside historians' thought and consciousness. The locus of historical reality is not in the mind of the historian but in the past events in which the historian had no say or hand; the historian only tries to build an account of the past and he 'creates' history only up to that point. The task of the historian is quite distinct from that of the fiction writer; whereas fiction writer describes reality in the sense of 'what could have happened', the historian is concerned with 'what did Happen'.

At this point it is necessary to draw the distinction between the two levels in which history is viewed by historians. History does "stand either for what happened or was done in the past (call this 'history') or for the study of it (call this 'history'). In the former sense history is the historian's subject matter, in the latter it is his study of it". (R.F. Atkinson, *Knowledge and explanation in History*, London 1978, p.9). Keeping this distinction in mind is important, but overstressing this distinction is unnecessary because there is no dichotomy between the two. The relationship between history as event and history as account is the normal relationship that obtains in all branches of knowledge between the subject matter of study and the study itself. In other words, this distinction between the two levels of history, $history_1$ and $history_2$ of Atkinson, and their mutual relationship are not specific to history alone but are universal.

Before we take up the central assumption around which revolve all the main issues relating to historical reality and knowledge, the assumption that historical reality is knowable, for analysis, it is worth noting the distinction between the two levels in which the concept of knowledge can be viewed. Knowledge can be regarded either as experience or as expression, the former is the process of reception and the latter is the process of communication. When we speak of a discipline what we mean by it is that it is an accepted body of knowledge at the expression level, a collection of statements. Knowledge at the experience level only provides the primary raw material, the source, the data on the basis of which knowledge as expression, which is identical with discipline, grows. This distinction between experience and expression is again universal to all disciplines and not specific to history.

The validity of the proposition that historical reality is knowable has been widely challenged; Descartes is not the only philosopher to have done it. As a recent example may be cited Bertrand Russell. Arguments based on universal scepticism which question the possibility of knowledge *per se* need not detain us because they question all disciplines and not specifically historical knowledge. Historian is not obligated to answer this kind of universal nihilism. Moreover, usually theories that advocate universal scepticism, or those which consider all perceived knowledge as illusory, posit them at the transcendental level and not at the empirical, holding that the empirical reality, though false and unreal in the ultimate sense, is allright at the empirical level. The working historian would be quite satisfied with the validity of historical reality at the empirical level.

"There is no logical impossibility in the hypothesis that the world sprang into being five minutes ago, exactly as it then was, with a population that 'remembered' a wholly unreal past. There is no logically necessary connection between events at different times; therefore nothing that is happening now or will happen in the future can disprove the hypothesis that the world began five minutes ago. Hence the occurrences which are called knowledge of the past are logically independent of the past; they are wholly analysable into present contents which might theoretically, be just what they are even if no past had existed". (Bertrand Russell, *The Analysis of Mind*, London 1921, pp. 159-60) What of course is meant by Russell in this startling assertion of five minute old origin of the world is that the present can, and in fact it ought to, stand unconcerned with the past as the past does not influence our present conditions in any way. It has been, however, demonstrated by Danto how patently misconceived such a notion can be. (A.C. Danto, *Analytical Philosophy of History*, Cambridge 1965, pp. 63ff). In our everyday life in hundreds of ways we are dependent on the carrying over of the past; our very structures of thought and language are teeming with past-referring concepts and terms. As Danto has pointed out that a word like 'father' or an expression like 'is a scar' are past-referring. To describe one as a father is to imply some past action or activities without which one would not have become a father. Similarly a scar implies a past wound. Past therefore is a concrete reality and not an illusory memory.

An argument that is often advanced, and apparently there is some force in the argument, against the validity of historical knowledge is that what purports to be historical reality is not actually what happened in the past but only an interpretation of it by historians. Michael Oakeshott, for example, argues that what happened is really not identical with that evidence forces us to believe. (Michael Oakeshott, *Experience and its Modes*, Cambridge 1933, pp. 94-100). This argument of Professor Oakeshott seems to have two underlying assumptions: (a) that the evidence in some way falsifies the reality or that the evidence erects a barrier which the historian fails to penetrate and reach the reality, (b) the evidence can allow us only a partial and not the total view of past. While historians would readily concede the latter of these assumptions, they would stoutly contest the earlier one. In fact, a major part of historical research methodology is directed to this very objective, i.e., examining and establishing the authenticity of evidence. No evidence is taken by the historian at its face value; a piece of evidence is put under rigorous investigation before it is used. Research methods are getting more and more advanced and refined and the ability of the historian to determine the dependability of his evidence is increasing day by day. (For discussion on some of the more recent methods of historical analysis and interpretation see Felix Gilbert and Stephen R Graubard ed. *Historical Studies Today*, New York 1972; Jerzy Topolski, *Methodology of History*, especially parts Five and Six: Richard E Beringer, *Historical Analysis---Contemporary Approaches to Clio's Craft*, New York 1978). In view of these it is impossible to accept the assumption of Prof. Oakeshott unless the argument is raised to the super agnostic level that all evidence *ipso facto* falsify reality, that an image is only an image and not the reality. A common historian's mind can not soar to the dizzy height where all disciplines evaporate.

We have stated above that historians would agree with the second of the above assumptions that the evidence would not allow a complete view of the past. Historians do not make the pretentious claim on behalf of their discipline that it is the embodiment of the whole truth. But this does not make the historian's work unworthy or superfluous. Reacting sharply to this kind of innuendo Elton wrote These opinions ... forget that inability to know all the truth is not the same thing as total inability to know the truth" (Elton, *op.cit.*, p. 51).

What really is held against historical knowledge is the allegedly necessary subjectivism that comes into play in writing history. The accusation of subjectivism has not been made by non-historians alone. Even some historians agree that historical account is dependent on historians relation with his subject of study. Charles beard is regarded as the foremost spokesman of the school of relativist historians. He adopted the position that writing history is not a quest in objective fact-finding but the declaration of an article of faith by the historian. "...any written history involves the selection of a topic and an arbitrary delimitation of its boarders... Within the boarders arbitrarily established, there is selection and organization of the facts by the process of thought. The selection and organization–a single act–will be controlled by the historians frame of reference composed of things deemed necessary and of things deemed desirable ... Whatever its nature the frame is inexorably there, in the mind... History moves around in a kind of cycle. History moves in a line, straight or spiral, and in some direction. The historian may seek to escape these issues by silence or by a confession of avoidance or he may face them boldly, aware of the intellectual and moral perils inherent in any decision -- in his act of faith". (Charles A Beard, 'Written History as an Act of Faith' in Hans Meyerhoff ed. *The philosophy of History in our time*, New York 1959, p. 151).

Beard's fears are obviously exaggerated. That a large body of determinate, hard and objective facts are available to historians is conceded even by Carl L Becker, himself a relativist like Beard. (Carl L Becker "What are Historical Facts?' in Meyerhoff, *op.cit.*, pp. 120-137). That in the Battle of Panipat Babar defeated the Lodi Sultan of Delhi is an example of such a determinate fact. In the area of determinate facts there is clearly no scope of subjectivism. And the mere fact of selecting a smaller area for work by the historian within a larger area covered by determinate hard facts would not take away its factual basis and render it arbitrary and imaginative.

Beard's contention that the selection of a topic and the delimitation of its boundary by the historian introduces a subjective element contains a veneer of truth. But this has very little real bearing on the question of historical reality. An example might help elucidate our point. Fishing rights over the river that flowed near our village home in our childhood used to be auctioned among fishermen . The river thus used to be parcelled out among different combines of fishermen and each group of fishermen used to put up boundary marks around the portion of the river allotted to them for fishing. While crossing the river by boat, a number of times as a child, I vividly remember, we occassionally used to come across the floating boundary marks made of long rows of bamboo poles tied to each other which were put up by the fishermen. These boundary marks did add to be visuals of the river in some minor ways but they never materially affected the complexion of the river or its image -- the river never appeared artificially or arbitrarily divided. the unity of the river remained perfectly clear despite the floating boundary marks.

Moreover, even in the interpretative area of a given historical work the acceptability or the unacceptability of the interpretation depends on its determinate factual basis. Historical interpretation is neither arbitrary nor imaginative but is based on reason, correspondence and coherence -- correspondence and coherence with the body of knowledge already existing in the field. (See Morton White, 'Can History be Objective?' in Meyerhoff, ed. *op.cit.*, pp. 188-202; Maurice Mandelbaum, *The Problem of Historical Knowledge*, New York, 1971, pp. 177-202; W.H. Walsh, *An Introduction to Philosophy of History*, London 1977, pp. 72-92). Cross checking and verification of data had always been the most important aspect of the methodology of history ever since the time of Herodotus and Thucydides. (R.G. Collingwood, *The Idea of History*, Oxford University Press 1951, p. 25; Trygve R Tholfsen, *Historical Thinking*, New York, 1967, pp. 21-23) That the historical methodology and explanation are used in disciplines other than history also surely points to the fact that the method is regarded to be useful and dependable also by those who do not have any professional stake in history. ('Equally, we find the thing I have described as historical explanation in many other places than history: in courts of law, in journalistic accounts, in the various social sciences. Historical explanation, in the rather limited sense of an action accounted for by referring to the agent's purpose and the like, is not limited to historians'. Rex Martin, *Historical Explanation*,

Cornell University Press, Ithaca and London, 1977, p. 15).

Another variation of the same argument is the theory that what passes for historical reality is not a discovery of past but only a construction or constitution of accounts of past. This constructionist or constitutionist theory has been forcefully advocated recently by J.W. Meiland and L.J. Goldstein. (J.W. Meiland, *Skepticism and Historical Knowledge*, New York 1965, L.J. Goldstein *op.cit.*) There is nothing wrong in history being what has been termed by Meiland as construction and Goldstein as constitution. All knowledge, whatever the kind, whenever is transmitted from the level of experience to the level of expression assumes the form of a construction. What passes for scientific knowledge for that matter is nothing but a construction from data. Historical account of past does not become suspect just because it is a construction or constitution.

A historian is usually aware of the fact that what he sets out to do is not merely narrating the event as it happened; he aspires for something more, he also tries to understand and explain besides narrating. The historian does not regard his task to be just a mechanical reproduction of the past but also to be an aid to illuminate it. From this point of view the historical knowledge is also a construction or constitution. But it must be made clear that this 'constitution' is not a contrivance; it is not introducing something from above which was not there, it is only making explicit what lay implicit. In mathematics nobody would take exception to giving in addition to the result, 2 x 2 = 4, the process and the logic through which the result is arrived at. Nobody would call it a contrivance. In history on the other hand any attempt at explanation is viewed with suspicion which is actually quite uncalled for which smacks of either ignorance or perversity.

The scepticism regarding the possibility of historical knowledge really centres around the argument that since the past is not available for direct observation hence there is no method of scientifically verifying the authenticity of historical accounts. There are a number of assumptions that lie under this argument which do not appear to be very satisfactory. The first assumption is that no knowledge is valid unless conclusions are drawn from controlled data in laboratory conditions. This assumption if accepted in totality would not only militate against all branches of social sciences but also against a substantial amount of scientific knowledge (Walsh, *op.cit*, p 31). A large number of sciences like geology and paleolontology have to depend to a large extent on memory-data. "The natural sciences have, it would seem, virtually abandoned the concepts of truth and falsehood; phenomena once regarded as objectively true are now seen to be only a statistical abstraction from random variables, and the accusing finger of the uncertainty principle further insists that, since observation alters a phenomenon, nothing is capable of being studied except after it is changed from the state in which it was meant to have been investigated. Practising scientists have therefore permitted the philosopher to remove the word true from their vocabulary and to substitute some such phrase as more probable, more accurately descriptive, more aesthetically or intellectually satisfying. This has not stopped scientists from continuing their efforts to investigate and understand nature, and in so far as it has reduced their positivist pride in the possession of the only strictly based truth the new philosophy may be thought of as gain. But historians have always been inclined to doubt the value, even the possibility, of their studies; they require not the new humility preached in the wake of Heisenberg, but some return to the assurance of the nineteenth century that the work they are doing deals with reality". (Elton, *op.cit.* p. 52). Although we would not agree with Elton that historians do not need to feel that they are dealing with reality, it is difficult not to agree with him in what he says about the limitations of natural science model as the only valid one for any quest of knowledge.

The second assumption of the above argument is that the absence of the direct observation facility is the same as the absence of authenticity. Direct observation constitutes a very limited range of experience and knowledge. We are vastly dependent as far as knowledge is concerned on sources other than direct observation. That the knowledge of past is based on memory-testimony is a truism that is repeated so often that it tends to obscure the fact that a very great deal of knowledge pertaining to 'present' is derived from similar or same source. "Of course, statements about past events may be supported by evidence or testimony; and in this regard may be felt to be in no worse case than the many statements about the present reporting events or state of affairs which are spatially beyond the range of direct observation. For example, 'It is raining in the hills' (on the basis of black clouds which can be seen from a distance or 'It is raining in London' (on the basis of a radio news bulletin). Statements about the present are not invariably founded upon direct observation, so that, even if it be thought that observation is invariably more reliable than indirect evidence (which is doubtful), it would not follow that statements about the past are necessarily less credible than those about the present" (Atkinson, *op.cit.* p. 45). In view of this it is curious that the readiness to believe reports relating to unobserved present is found much more than the readiness to believe unobserved past.

It might be mentioned here in passing that there is a commonly held notion among non-historians that all historical evidence, since they all come from past, belong to the same category as far as their temporal positions are concerned. This is not true. Evidence in relation to a particular event being studied by the historian can be either (a) 'before' or (b) 'contemporaneous" or (c) "after'. Normally it is considered uncritically that the contemporaneous is the most authentic because it reflects the present observation. But the case is not always that simple and direct observation is not the best guide or most illuminating. The reality of an event is sometimes contingent upon what has gone before; Mark Anthony's celebrated funeral speech would not have become what it was without Caesar's assassination. The converse is also sometimes true, the reality of an event becomes clear only in the light of subsequent events. The fall of Bastille, for example, marked the beginning of the French Revolution. These aspects of reality would not be visible through direct observation alone. In other words direct observation divorced from temporal sequence can lead to distortion of reality. (A.C. Danto, *Analytical Philosophy of History*, Cambridge, 1965, ch. VIII).

It is also necessary to speak of the notion of significance in history. The sceptics of historical knowledge have often levelled the charge that since historians are guided by the notion of significance in the selection of their material they are guilty of subjectivism. It is true that the notion of significance is a relative concept; a fact is significant in relation to something (a fact or series of facts). But it also must be remembered that the notion of significance is not an irrational sentiment, it has rational basis founded on hard logic. A fact would not become significant by somebody merely wishing it. Moreover, the notion of significance is not specific to history alone, it has important role in all disciplines.

Difference of opinion among historians has been the most commonly cited illustration of the falliability of historical knowledge and explanation. That historians are notoriously fond of controversies and debates is too well known. It is also perhaps the most visible and eye-catching of all the aspects of the historians' activities for the public. But what is usually lost sight of in the thick fog of seemingly interminable controversies is the steadily increasing body of agreed historical knowledge which is the very product of differences of opinion among historians. This is what finally matters most and this is were the validity of historical knowledge lies.

Historian's job, as we have remarked above, is to build an account of past. And building an account involves not only making a mechanical reproduction of an isolated individual fact but also making statements about the why and how of that fact; in other words an account also includes explanation. Since events are bound together in temporal and causal relationships, historical narration of an event has to describe, in order to make the meaning of that event clear, that event in its relationship with other events. Historical account therefore is not so much a description of 'events' as the description of a process or processes. One therefore finds it difficult to agree with Raymond Aron, despite the great sophistication of his arguments, that historical research ought to be confined to the study of single facts and their causes leaving the task of working out the general relationships to the sociologists. ("... historical research sticks to the antecedents of a singular fact, sociological research to the causes of a fact which may be repeated". Raymond Aron, *Introduction to the philosophy of History*, London 1961, p. 226). Aron's thesis, , however, is self contradictory. The moment one looks historically for the causes of a single fact one is inevitably led into the matrix of historical process.

Finally, a historical fact is not only related causally and temporarily with other historical facts but it is also spatially related to other facts in a given society. A historical fact is also a societal fact.

"What is the relation between societal facts and historical facts? At any rate it is obvious that every historical fact, whether simple or complex, is a societal fact, the more so if we realize that ... only the past and future exist, where as the present is a conventional concept. Hence it would be covered by the definition formulated by S Czarnowski and stating that a societal fact is a fact which 'in its origin, process, or outcome is conditioned by the existence of a human community'. Thus, for instance, the death of Napoleon I, like the death of any other person, is a societal (and a historical) fact, because we are concerned here not just with a biological fact of death of a human being, but with the death of a person who had a surname, a first name, a profession or trade, etc., and thus was a member of a given community. Every societal fact is also historical in the sense that it is a product of development.

This kind of 'historicity' is inherent in any societal fact. But a societal fact need not be historical, if it is examined only as an element of social structure, without consideration of the development factor.

In conclusion it may be said that the concept of historical fact requires the consideration of both its place in a structure and its role in the process of change." (Jerzy Topolski, *Methodology of History*, Warsaw 1976, pp. 224-25).

The historical reality in the view of historians is a dynamic entity and the function of the historian, even if it is not explicitly stated by every historian, ultimately is to elucidate the nature of this dynamic entity.

REFERENCES

Aron, Raymond, *Introduction to the Philosophy of History*, Weidenfeld and Nicolson ; London, 1961.

Atkinson, R.F , *Knowledge and Explanation in History*, The Macmillan Press; London 1968.

Beard, Charles A., 'Written History as an Act of Faith' in Hans Meyerhoff(ed.) *The Philosophy of History in our Time.*

Becker, Carl L., 'What are Historical Facts?' in Meyerhoff, *op.cit*.

Beringer, Richard E., *Historical Analysis --- Contemporary Approaches to Clio's Craft*, John Wiley & Sons; New York 1978.

Cellingwood, R.G., *The Idea of History*, Clarendon Press; Oxford, 1951.

Danto, A.C., *Analytical Philosophy of History*, Cambridge University Press; Cambridge, 1965.

Elton, G.R., *The Practice of History*, Sydney University Press; London, 1967.

Gilbert, Felix, and Graubard, Stephen R., (ed.) *Historical Studies Today*, W.W. Norton Company; New York, 1972.

Goldstein, Leon J., *Historical Knowing*, University of Texas Press; Austin & London, 1976.

Lakatos, Imre, and Musgrave, Alan, (ed.) *Criticism and Growth of Knowledge*, Cambridge University Press Cambridge, 1970.

Mandelbaum, Maurics, *The Problem of Historical Knowledge*, Books for Libraries Press; New York, 1971.

Martin, Rex, *Historical Explanation*, Cornell University Press; Ithacs and London, 1977.

Masterman, Margaret, 'The Nature of a Paradigm' in Imre Lakaton and Alan Musgrave, *op.cit*.

Meiland, J.W., *Skepticism and Historical Knowledge*, Random House; New York, 1965.

Meyerhoff, Hans, *et.al The Philosophy of History in Our Time*, Doubleday and Company; New York, 1959.

Oakeshott, Michael, *Experience and Ita Modes*, Cambridge University Press; Cambridge, 1933.

Plumb, J.H., *The Death of the Past*, London, 1969.

Russell, Bertrand, *The Analysis of Mind*, George Allen and Unwin; London, 1921.

Tholfsen, Trygve, *Historical Thinking*, Harper & Row; New York, 1967.

Topolski, Jerzy, *Methodology of History*, D. Reidel Publishing Company, Boston and PWN Polish Scientific Publisher, Warsaw, 1976.

White, Morton, 'Can History Be Objective? In Meyerhoff, *op.cit.*

Walsh, W.H., *An Introduction to Philosophy of History*, Hutchinson of London, London, 1977.

SEVEN

Om Prakash

PERCEPTION OF SOCIAL REALITY AND HISTORY

Perception and reality are familiar categories or degrees of knowledge in the domain of philosophy. Reality may be a product of perception integrated by reason but all perception is not necessarily real.[1] What is real is understood in contradistinction to what is illusory or phenomenal.[2] Whether this philosophical view of reality is compounded of perceptions alone impinging on mind which is a *tabula rasa* or also of something a *priori* inherent in mind besides reason as well is a great philosophical question. When philosophy talks of perception[3], it leaves no perception out. When it talks of reality, it similarly allows nothing to stand out of its definition of it which is all inclusive. Yet it distinguishes several levels of reality, e.g., illusory, phenomenal and ultimate.

In spite of some overlapping, social reality is not equivalent to philosophical reality, nor is it all-inclusive like the latter. The phenomenal reality of the philosopher includes not only social reality but also natural phenomena. Social reality, however, is confined to the social space alone. Arising from perception which is the common source of all knowledge, phenomenal reality of the natural world is studied by science. Phenomenal reality of the human world forms the subject-matter of social sciences, e.g., sociology, psychology, political science, economics, etc., and retrospectively of history. What is presented in the form of literature, myth, and religion, is not probably social reality proper but the ethos of social, individual and moral values, norms and aesthetics-a middle zone where the domains of human activities and Nature interpenetrate.[4] Devoted as this study is to the consideration of this circumscribed view of perception and social reality in the further restricted domain of history, we have to distinguish from perception in general the perception of historical facts, on the one hand, and from the conception of social reality, in general, that of historical social reality, on the other.

As an instrument of perceiving social reality, history originated when it was harnessed by Herodotus to the task of reconstructing, in the most authentic manner, the glorious victory of the Hellenes over the mighty Persians in the fifth century B.C. It was proclaimed as a victory of ancient Greek democracy over Achaemenid despotism, of determination over brute force, of military skill over the power of mere numbers and of the Hellenic way of life over that of the Oriental.[5] Christian historiographers used this device to perceive through the events of the past the Divine plan and the truths of the scripture and pious intuition. This view of the past proved a strong counterblast to the brute force and organised violence which the Roman empire represented at its best, and the steep moral degradation and repeated humiliation by barbarian hordes, at its worst. Its fall was interpreted as the well-deserved Divine punishment it merited while the phenomenal rise of Christianity was viewed as only too fitting a reward of the Roman atrocities braving by the meek and non-violent Christians who had nothing but the weapons of Faith and moral fortitude to fight them.[6] History in the hands of the Christians was called upon to vindicate this heroic struggle of the good against the evil, of Faith against Paganism and of meekness against brutality, and the ultimate victory of the former over the latter. History was again used by the Renaissance historians as an effective instrument for perceiving that the creation is older than Bible, that man is more important than religion and that reason is greater than Faith.[7] Ascendancy of reason by the eighteenth century, however, painted in blackest colours the Age of Faith and produced an attitude of uncompromising scepticism towards all religious myths and legends.[8] This prejudice was again perceived by the thinkers of the Romantic movement, and history played its role in detecting things of value even in the discarded heaps of the products of Faith, spontaneity and unreason. It could show that everything was not dark and decadent in the Middle Ages and that the 'noble savage' was not less important than the civilised man proud of reason. Like the Original Sin of the Bible, reason had only destroyed the pristine purity of man and has only contributed to his fall and thraldom. Back to Nature was the call given by the Romanticists, which history was called upon to authenticate.[9] This led to anthropologisation of history in the nineteenth century. Archaeologists too contributed their utmost to the further glamourisation of the past. The cross-currents of individualism, socialism, scientism, idealism, and empiricism, added to the complexities of historical perception[10] of the historical social reality, and for the first time in the history of history, the question of the character of history and historical perception was raised. This led to the formulation of a new subject called philosophy of history and our present exercise too is an attempt at identifying the naure of historical perception in contradistinction to and in complementarity with that of other instruments of perceiving social reality. The other aspect of the problem, that of the nature of historical reality has been taken up by Dr Sibesh Bhattarcharya in his contribution to this volume.

Theoretically, social sciences other than history are to take into account all the facts of the social space and try to integrate them into social reality of their own. But history does not even theoretically take into account all facts pertaining to past. Of these, it selects only the historical ones and leaves the rest, and the picture of social reality it draws on the basis of them is not quite the same as the sociologist, the psychologist, the economist, or the political scientist brings out. The sociological generalisations emanate from the perception of a living situation whereas historical conclusions are derived from surviving memories and traces of a situation which existed sometimes in the past. Historian's perception of the situation is, therefore, necessarily indirect and his generalisations and explanations can contribute the least to the venture of social engineering. Distinguishing historical facts from the rest has also an inevitable reference to initial inquiry and that, in turn, to something *a priori*. The relation of historical social reality to this *a priori*, on the one hand, and to social reality, in general, and the social reality in history arrived at *a posteriori*, on the other, is again to be discussed.

Historical facts, their perception or apperception

What is a historical fact? All the facts contained in the sources of a historian are not his historical facts, or all that has happened in the past is also not necessarily included by him in the category of historical facts. A historian always selects his own facts from a welter of them. Historical facts, therefore, differ not only from the facts of a sociologist, a psychologist or a political scientist but also from historian to historian. Their choice depends on the nature of the initial inquiry which a historian assigns to himself. Apart from the quest of the usual units of history, viz., "greatmen, peoples, eras, institution" and also apart from the attempt to "know what is universal in history" or to "derive the general in the sequence of the particular events",[11] historians at times also seek to discover the 'idea', the hand of God, the supra-individual causalities and processes, the cultural milieu, on the spiritual side, and the inbuilt contradictions of various modes of production, the dialectical motion, and the ideal of classless society, on the material side.[12] What is there at the root of such passionate pronouncements about the theme of history as "stop giving us heroes and tyrants, stop describing mortal lives from cradle to the grave, stop searching for what motivated the individual. Give us the life of the masses, their toil and suffering, their hopes and their delusions, their passions and their violent deeds."[13] Though, according to Huizinga, "the question of whether the individual or the group makes history is logically unanswerable and is irrelevant for the historian,"[14] such thematic shifts in the quest of history do originate from the shifts in our present day scale of values. The questions put to the past are necessarily projections of important issues of the present. Such issues do carry with them a certain prior view of social reality and change which our direct perception of things and current theories about them generate among us.

Thus we do not approach the past with a mind all clean having nothing but the faculty of reason in it. Historical social reality is created not from simple perception of facts as contained in the sources of history but from that of a select body of historical facts chosen on the basis of a prior understanding of issues denoting a value or a set of values.[15] Historical knowledge ensues from a process of analysis and synthesis of these select data which may be proclaimed as the work of reason. What reason does in social sciences is to reduce particulars into general patterns and processes, an understanding of which may help an attempt at social and political engineering. Social reality thus arrived at corresponds to Weber's "ideal types" with which the actual may be contrasted.[16] The actual is thus not the same as the real in the context of social sciences.[17] Does reason play the same role in history? Does it analyse or synthesise the perception of the select historical facts to derive "ideal types" or does it bring out the actual? The Positivistic and Marxist programmes assign the former task to history while historicism, starting from Ranke,[18] ascribes the latter to it. In the first the particular is reduced to the general and history virtually substantiates the theories of sociology or Marxism while, in the second, stress is shifted from the constants in the course of events, to events themselves, and whatever instruction, principle or pattern history is to impart is reflected in the specific context of the events without any conscious effort to discover them.[19] Though the particular becomes meaningful in the context of the general, the general by no means appears to be the upshot of history, for historical generalization can never attain the level of such hypotheses as can absolutely determine the nature and behaviour of the particular. Emphasis on events and the specific context helps to recreate the actual rather than the real or the "ideal types".[20] A search for "ideal types", "laws", patterns and processes in the perceived historical facts amounts to a futile excercise, if the same quest has initially conditioned the selection of facts to be perceived. Perception here turns out to be apperception and the initial inquiry a virtual construct of history with a modern value or a set of modern values placed at the top of the whole excercise in the form of a theory-oriented initial question.

Perception of the need to write history

What does, for example, the question about the makers of history indicate? Does it indicate a change in the awareness of the historian as the result of his personal experience of the age he lives in or an impact on him of the intellectual fashion of looking at the understanding of recent developments? What kind of perception is this? It is at the stress of the necessity of such a perception that the die of history is cast. This perception, in fact, decides the nature of the intuitive *a priori* of the historian which turns the perception and selection of historical facts into an act of apperception. This kind of perception may be described as the perception of the problem and it may be said to arise when the foregoing historical excercises leave something unresolved or unexplained.[21] The greatmen theory of history certainly did not adequately explain the role of people in the making of history, which simply did not strike the formulators of the great men theory of history because they had never seen the people playing an important part in the running screen of happenings before their eyes. Bringing the people to the fore still left out the role of the logic of the situation unexplained and this brought about the study of conditioning factors and their predictability. Historical research thus has its own inherent mode of progression in which the present of the historian, i.e., his awareness and understanding of the present besides those of the past play no less important a part. But the difficulty arises when the discarded theories are still adhered to and when finality is claimed for theories leaving many things palpably unexplained. Then it appears that the historian, instead of being guided by his own perception of the problematic situation, is swayed by some dogmatic preferences and prejudices in not conceding to his successors the privilege of putting to critical test the explanations and solutions offered by him. It is only in such a situation that historical research loses its independence and becomes a handmade of some theory or theoretical construct.[22]

Difficulty also arises when the newly discovered makers of history are painted in brightest colours putting their predecessors on the stage into the Satanic role of a villain. Thus, with the accession of the people on the stage of history, there started a tendency of attributing all their miseries to the kings and nobles who headed the class of their exploiters. All their heroic struggles are waged against these who created situations of extreme suffering and injustice by their sinister designs. The theme of empire building gets substituted by the story of production and extraction of surplus with the result that the previously perceived forces of justice and fairplay are turned into those of discrimination and tyranny. The symbol of justice and security, the state, itself becomes essentially anti-people. Similarly, the issue between spiritualism and materialism also tends to stress the primacy of ideological or economic factor above all else. The stages of economic developments or epochs do not neatly fit in the chronological segments conceived on the basis of political events, and create a confusion in the scheme of periodization, on the one hand, and turn some time brackets into ones animated by the controversy about their golden or dark character, on the other.[23] How are we to view the character of the Middle Ages and especially of cities in it. Are they the survivals of Antiquity, 'islands in the seas of village life', or are they the seedlings of the renaissance?[24] Is feudalism a universal or purely an European phenomenon? Do we have models of Antiquity and Middle Ages, slavery and feudalism in India? Such problems as are agitating the minds of historians at present probably do not originate from their perception of the problematic situation necessitating an adequate explanation of something left unexplained by their predecessors. Much of the heat is generated by the question of modern preferences, values and 'isms' involved, which overshadows the critical faculty and does not allow it to examine their uncritically appropriated premises.

Selection of facts with regard to the necessity of the problematic situation critically perceived hardly breeds any further necessity to choose from among the various value-laden theories or 'isms'. But when it is not there the balance swings to the other extreme of casting history in the mould of an epic or drama, having more regard for climax and anti-climax, contrasts and effects than for the problem to be solved. Facts are made a vehicle of all this. This kind of perception of the need to write history creates only a rationalised modern myth in the garb of history and is hardly more than a piece of propaganda.[25] The second kind of the necessity is to be clearly distinguished from the first, as it exceeds the bounds of perception and walks into the domain of apperception issuing out of an acquired *a priori* grafted into one's conscience rather than emerging from a critical appraisal of the received situation.

History and social history

The foregoing discussion shows that proper history is always born out of a critical perception of a problematic situation in historiography. What kind of knowledge does this history create? One answer to this question is that it creates the solution of the problems it raises. The problem pertains to the knowledge of the past as required in the context of the present. Therefore, the whole past is not relevant to history simultaneously, some particular aspects of it alone are made relevant from time to time and exposed to the focus of the historical research impelled by the need of study and the change of the perspective before the eyes or mind's eyes of the practising historian. The purpose of history is neither to re-create the past, nor to discover the laws of events or human behaviour, nor still to unravel the organizational and functional modes of social, political, economic or other institutions and processes. The purpose of history is contained in the question why do we look to the past and the kind of knowledge history supplies is strictly in accordance with our expectations from the past. Do we look to past in order to get the knowledge called social reality? Has it a reference to the present or to the past or to both?

We have seen above that the social reality of a sociologist, a psychologist or an economist differs necessarily from that of a historian. History is neither a substitute nor an appendix, nor still a raw-material for these. If the actual is to be distinguished from the real and if history is confined to describing events of the past as they actually happened, then history may have nothing to do with social reality. But there can be no doubt that while writing history, the historian is necessarily dealing with the social phenomenon into his own frame of reference. The knowledge produced by him cannot be altogether divorced from social phenomenon by any play of words and concepts. Call it reality or not, it is social and at the same time historical, a bridge between the present and the past. If may not tell you the secrets of social institutions, functional or behavioural, once for all, but it is also not wholly without them. It may not help you in formulating general and universal laws of social action or social formations produced around certain theories of production or else in discovering "ideal types" which may not wholly conform to what is obtaining in the actual and yet be true and real, as it studies segments of constant flux produced by innumerable actions and reactions causes and effects, conditions and conditioned that join the present with the past. General and particular, actual and real represent only two of the numerous polarities included into this unfathomable richness of history. Social reality, when viewed in terms of exclusive generality, presents probably only one side of the coin of which the missing side is supplied by the actual. History is capable of presenting both simultaneously in their natural union of the event. That is why it does not fully conform to the requirements of the mould of any theory. It blasts all definitions of social reality, rendering them to be only generally true.

Social reality can be defined either on the pattern of philosophical, reality or on that of scientific reality. Philosophically, reality may be conceived in Absolute terms representing, at the same time, the supreme value. Its relation with the world of appearance is variously conceived in terms of different theories of logic and causation. Scientifically, reality represents the truest of all knowledge which may or may not be different from appearance. The test of scientific reality is a perfect and never failing explanation to be verified experimentally or under controlled modes of observation.[26] The scientific view of causality lasts till it is experimentally falsified and given up in favour of a fresh one.

Social reality cannot be Absolute in the manner of philosophical reality nor can it represent the supreme value. But, following the philosophical method, it can be recognised with reference to norms and values enshrined in a social system. There can be no question of perfect and never-failing causal predictability in social reality nor can there be experimental verifiability in social matters. Yet proceeding scientifically as far as possible, one can no doubt identify social reality in terms of social system. But is the digestive system the sole reality of man? Or else the norms and values of his behaviour represent the totality of reality about him? These analogies make it quite clear that such identifications of social reality are inadequate and partial. The sole contribution of history to the problem in question lies in its demonstrating this fact. The question of the area of history being real or actual does not arise, as it clearly transcends this dichotomy and points to the limitations of such a dichotomy.

Complementarity of historical perception

This is not to argue that historical perception is absolutely autonomous and stands in no need of reciprocity with other kinds of perception of the social reality. How history needs a sociological perspective would be evident if one were to write a history of caste, ignoring the perspective of sociological surveys available in the form of modern Census Reports. A history of caste based on *dharmasastras* and other literary sources alone would be like a history of

Asoka written without taking into account the data of his inscriptions. The normative picture of the social order thus gathered would be lacking even the anticipated substratum of social reality. The simplistic and inadequate character of the traditional origin theory of caste through mixed marriages **cutting across Varna** lines could be detected only when the complexity of the process of the formation of castes in recent times was highlighted as the result of these comprehensive surveys. The sociological perspective thus complements the historical perception of social reality.

An attempt to understand caste retrospectively as a deduction of mere sociological principles, subordinating the historical perspective to them, also produces distortions like the ones visible in the **Homo Hierarchicus** of Dumont. In a historical critique[28] of this bold attempt, I have elsewhere shown that approaches like this fail to relate the so-called system of ideas and values obtruding upon the consciousness of the observer to the general ethos and telos of the culture in the totality of which alone they acquire appropriate meaning and order of precedence and preference, failing which the interpretative task is left entirely to the competence and mercy of the researcher. He may turn the scale of values upside down depending on his own arbitrary impressions of the importance of one value over the other, or include in the category of value what is not at all a value. Unless, therefore, the historical dimension surviving in the present as the spirit of its inherited culture is not adequately taken into account, the sociological perception of the social reality is likely to fall a victim of a distorted view by virtue of reading the present into the past.

Impressionistic views of social reality computed of ones intuitive understanding of the present and the past sometimes turn out to be absurd and untenable on a closer observation of facts. An example in point is an observation of the Supreme Court in the case of Balaji versus Mysore State.[29] In this case the backwardness of a caste or social group was required to be determined not by its relative backwardness from the forward castes or social groups but by a difference of at least 50 per cent between its own standard and the average standard of the State. On closer scrutiny the Mandal Commission have found that this principle in actual circumstances leads to absurd results. According to 1971 Census, they have pointed out,

80 per cent of the population of Bihar was illeterate which is the average proportion of illiteracy in the State. In order to be determined as educationally backward a caste or social group must necessarily have an illiterarcy percentage of 80+50 = 130 per cent which is absurd. The Indian average per capita yearly expenditure on living for the rural areas was Rs. 900.00 according to the prices of 1977-78. The line of poverty in that year stood at a per capita yearly expenditure of Rs. 780.00. The actual difference between the average per capita yearly expenditure on living and that on the line of poverty was 13.3 per cent . To make it 50 per cent for determining the economic backwardness of a social group or caste would require its yearly per capita income to fall below even the subsistence level which is absurd.[30]

A study in the behaviour of flattery and sycophancy conducted in the Psychology Department of the Allahabad University has concluded from its surveys that such a behaviour is risky in the Western society but it is not so in the Indian society. Psychology as a social science fails to offer an explanation of this difference and the researchers are looking forward for the same to history.31[31]

All these examples amply show that both history and social sciences stand in complementary relationship with each other. But the needs of this complementarity will be better answered if their mutual infiltration usually follows the line of methodology. Historians should however be on their guards against allowing methodology to become a substitute of substantial research. They should not, for example, extrapolate all the sociological generalisations about the nature of a tribal society while dealing with the social order of the early Vedic Age simply because tribes were there or while exploring the original sources focus their attention on what is expected in a tribal society only, ignoring all else and especially such pieces of evidence as are inconvenient and point to a different direction.

NOTES AND REFERENCES

1. "Usually Reality was considered the being of something to the exclusion of all the contingent in it, i.e., that which is not by necessity connected with the given being." Rosenthal, M. and Yudin, p. (1967), *A Dictionary of Philosophy*, Moscow, p. 380.

2. Medieval realism distinguished between nominalism and realism, materialism and idealism, *Ibid.* p. 379.

3. This is precisely the issue between Locke and Kant, empiricists and idealists.

4. Meinecke, F., "Values and Causalities in History" Stern, F., (1970), ed., *The Varieties of History From Voltair to the Present*, London, pp. 268-288.

5. "To the Greek historian, therefore, there could never be any such thing as a history of Greece. There could be a history of a fairly extensive complex of events, like the Persian War or the Peloponnesian War; but only on two conditions. First, this complex of events must be complete in itself: it must have a beginning, a middle and an end, like a plot of an Aristotelian tragidy. Secondly, it must be *evdvvonros*. like an Aristotelian city-state". Collingwood, (1963) *The Idea of History*, London, p. 27.

6. St. Augustine, The City of God, Barker's Introduction to its translation by him.

7. *Encyclopaedia Britannica*, Vol. 8, p. 952.

8. "The central point of history for these writers is the sunrise of the modern scientific spirit. Before that, everything was superstition and darkness, error and imposture. And of these things there can be no history, not only because they are unworthy of historical study, but because there is in them no rational or necessary development: the story of them is a tale told by an idiot, full of sound and fury, signifying nothing". Collingwood, *op. cit.* p. 80.

9. Rousseau, *Contract Social*, I. viii.

10. Ranke represents the watershed between the relatively less complex and more complex phases of modern historiography and philosophy of history. See Momigliano, A.(1966), "One hundred years after Ranke" quoted in

Blackurn, R.(ed.) (1975), *Ideology in Social Sciences*, Glasgow, p. 267.

11. Berr, H., "About Our Program" Stern, *op. cit.*, p. 252.

12. Meinecke, F., *op. cit.*, p. 269.

13. Huizinga, J., "The Idea of History" Stern, *op.cit.*, p. 298.

14. *Ibid.*, p. 299.

15. Carr, E.H. (1964), *What is History*, Penguine Books, p. 11.

16. Clapham, J. "The·Economic History as a Discipline", Stern, *op. cit.*, p. 311.

17. Such a distinction is also drawn in philosophy. See Rosenthal and Yudin, *op. cit.*, p. 380.

18. Ranke, "A Fragment from the 1830's", Stern, *op. cit.*, p. 59.

19. The four principles of Rankean approach to scientific history are: 1. objectivity of historical truth, 2. the priority of facts over concepts, 3. the equivalent uniqueness of all events, and 4. the centrality of politics. Kriger, L (1978), *Ranke: Meaning of History* as summarised in its review by Milton Convensky, *History Teacher*, Vol. XI, No. 4, pp. 393f.

20. Walsh, W.H. (1967), *An Introduction to the Philosophy of History*, London, p. 18.

21. Northrop, F.S.C. (1953), *The Logic of Science and Humanities*, New York, p. 17.

22. Walsh, *op. cit.*, pp. 26ff.

23. Huizinga calls this difficulty "the danger of stereo-types" *op. cit.*, pp. 29f.

24. Dobb, M. (1967), *Studies in the Development of Capitalism*, London, pp. 36, 42-43 and Hilton, (1947), R., *Modern Quarterly*, Vol. 2, No. 3, pp. 267f. Also Southern, *The Making of Middle Ages*, pp. 12f.

25. Huizinga, *op. cit.*, p. 292.

26. Northrop, *op. cit.*, p. 142.

27. Meinecke, *op. cit.*, p. 268.

28. Om Prakash, (1979) "Concept of Hierarchy and Power in the Ancient Indian Theory of Society and State", *Proceedings of the Indian History Congress*, Waltair, p. 54.

29. *A.I.R.* (1963), Supreme Court, 649.

30. *Backward Class Commission Report*, (1980), New Delhi, Vol. I, paras 11.20-11.32.

31. I am very much beholden to Prof. Janak Pandey for drawing my attention to this very significant example on the point.

EIGHT

Alok Rai

THE VIRUS THAT EXPLODED, OR, SEEING THROUGH THE PAPERS

... And so each venture
Is a new beginning, a raid on the inarticulate ....

T.S. ELIOT

Good prose is like a window pane.

GEORGE ORWELL

We have to cease to think if we refuse to do it in the prison-house of language ....

F.W. NIETZSCHE

Newspapers constitute a privileged discourse in any society. They are a key element in the ideological apparatus, an influential determinant in the process of signification wherein and whereby a society crystallises its meanings, learns to think about and so, see itself. The English language press of this country is not only a part of this privileged discourse, it is also, evid ntly, a discourse of the privileged. As such, it is of particular interest to anyone who in interested in the processes whereby social meanings are generated. Because of course, while all meanings might be equal, some are inevitably more so. And the ways in which the powerful understand reality are not merely matters of academic interest - these forms of understanding feed back into reality by becoming, in turn, the determinants of actions, policies, interventions.

My sample for this investigation consists of copies of all the national English language dailies published during the first ten days of 1982. The original impulse for this enquiry derives from Orwell's essay, 'Politics and the English Language'- more precisely, from Orwell's seminal insight that language is the terrain on which ideological conflicts are fought out. It is also implied, stretching the metaphor, that language is the strongest and subtlest weapon deployed in such conflicts. Thus, irrespective of whether language is seen as tool or terrain, it is presumed that a diligent examination of language is likely to reveal significant injury, alteration, detail. Finally, in order to provide a workable focus for my investigation, I have confined myself to the newspaper coverage of a single macabre event which took place, as it happens, on New Year's Eve, and so figured prominently in my newspaper sample - the killing of ten lower-caste women and children in a village in western U.P. The name of the village was variously described in the papers as Sarhupur or Sadhupur - it could never be established satisfactorily which of the two is correct so I have, arbitrarily, opted for the latter.

Newspapers are, unless one is especially careful, endowed with an alarming transparency. There is, so their unstated project runs, a world in which events happen, and these events are, faithfully, mapped into the ideologically neutral discourse of the newspaper. News consists of objectively available 'facts', reporters are value-free, and the language of the papers is a eunuch, unaffected and unmarked by the bordello in which it is employed. This used to be a powerful position in the past - but the news that the palace has been overrun might still take some time filtering down to the marketplace.

In academia, however, the recognition is becoming general that 'reality' is inherently formless, amorphous, and that it must therefore, and necessarily, be transformed, shaped, indeed, **formed** for human uses. Writing on 'Interpretation and the Sciences of Man', Charles Taylor has pointed out'... the artificiality of the distinction between social reality and the language of description of that social reality,[1] because, clearly, language is the primary means by which amorphous social reality is formed, endowed with contexts, rendered significant, made available for thought and action. An influential commentator on the processes of social signification, Stuart Hall, is categorical:

> The patterns of meanings imposed on events, the logics of arrangement and presentation, are not given in the raw material: even when events have a meaning of their own, those meanings are modified and sometimes transformed, when they enter an already formed discourse or linguistic 'space'.[2]

The meaning of Sadhupur is affected by whether it is the subject of a police investigation or a political pronouncement, a journalistic essay or an academic analysis of the various ways in which that meaning has been sought to be apprehended, and communicated.

The sophistication which we professionally, habitually, bring to bear upon the understanding of more obviously, self-consciously patterned forms of utterance, whether ly ric poetry or realistic fiction is, I believe, very much to our purpose here as well. Because the ordinariness of ordinary language is, after all, little more than the staleness of familiarity, which we need to shed in order to regard critically even avowedly 'literary' texts. As for the irreducible factuality of the world of newspapers, it provides no immunity from critical scrutiny. Not only is it the case that developments in documentary fiction, the fiction of fact sometimes called 'faction' - the examples which spring readily to mind are Truman Capote's **In Cold Blood** and Norman Mailer's **The Executioner's Song** - have destroyed any immunity that factuality might be said to provide. We have also suggested, above, that for reality to be constituted as 'facts' certain, specific, acts of attention and transformation are essential. One might recall at this point Paul Fussell's elegant demonstration that 'Our access to events, even so significant an event as the Great War, must be through the makers of plots - that is, poets ...'[3] Raymond Williams's warning to media analysts is apt and pointed. 'The fact that certain events have undoubtedly occurred,' he writes, should not be allowed 'to conceal or to override the equally evident fact that as they move from events to news they are being narrated, and that certain long-standing problems of narration - the identity of the narrator, his authority, his point of view, his assumed relationship to his readers or hearers, his possible wider purposes in selecting and narrating these events in this way - come inevitably into question'.[4] The tragic event in Sadhupur, therefore, is not my primary focus - it is, rather, the processes of signification through which that event has been sought to be understood. The killing of obscure individuals in an obscure place is, in a sense that is both punning and precise, merely the pretext for this, preliminary, enquiry.

The relationship between language and ideology must, clearly, be an intimate one. Language is ideology's necessary element, the primary substance in and through which the forms of ideology - its arguments and ideas, its perceptions and conceptions - are constituted. Thus, it is difficult to disagree with Fowler and Kress when they write:

> Language serves to confirm and consolidate the organisations which shape it, being used to manipulate people, to establish and maintain them in economically convenient roles and statuses, to maintain the power of state agencies ... this is effected partly by direct and indirect speech acts, partly by more generalised processes in which the theory or ideology of a culture or a group is linguistically encoded, articulated and tacitly affirmed.[5]

There are, however, a couple of important remarks to be made in this connection: firstly, whereas language is an insidious and subtle means whereby the dominance of the dominant is inscribed in the minds of their victims - Orwell buffs may recall here the tyranny of Newspeak in **Nineteen Eighty-Four** - it is inherent in the necessarily generalised availability of language that it can also be used, within institutional limitations, to subvert that dominance. In attempting to do that, however, and this is my second point, one is liable to come up against the real world - not merely the flat-footed but fully armed minion of the State whose violence is the ultimate sanction of the power which first appears linguistically encoded, but also crucially, the world of actuality itself, the solid, four-dimensional world which language both represents and articulates.

A happening out there, in reality so to speak, is really something like an orphan, a friendless and unloved child who arrives at Bombay V.T. in search of fortune and amnesia. It takes a little while before it can be 'adopted' for various legitimate and illegitimate purposes. The fact of the killings was announced, flatly, in the agency handouts which appeared on New Year's Day, nestling cheek by jowl with the bits and pieces from here and there about ringing out the old year, ringing in the new:

> A gang of outlaws shot dead 10 Harijans, including women and children, yesterday in Sadhupur village of Shikohabad tehsil of Mainpuri district.
>
> (TOI, l:lB)

The tone is bureaucratic, neutral, precise. Along with the basic information, one newspaper published, without comment, an item of information which may, arguably, be germane to an understanding of these macabre events:

> On learning about the fresh killings on New Year's Eve, Chief Minister Vishwanath Pratap Singh cancelled a scheduled Press conference and rushed to Delhi.
>
> (HT, 1:1B)

Not Sadhupur, Delhi - no doubt in search of consolation and enlightenment. The general response, among those who stayed, was that the crime was 'meaningless'. The Home Secretary declared: 'No motive can be discerned in the murders. It is an act of sheer madness'. (IE, l:lb). The Home Minister herself declared that the crime was 'mad', but then proceeded to adduce a reason for it: the arrest of the husband of the cousin sister of the prime suspect, Anar Singh. (HT, l:8H) Others also could not leave the unlovely orphan unappropriated for too long, and the papers reported 'Cong-I sources' which, without any awareness of paradox, were able to 'see the hidden hand of some caste-based Opposition party behind the killings of Harijans'. (HT, l:lC) This was a theme which grew stronger as the days passed. Meanwhile, it was interesting to observe a quaint use of the word 'motivated'. Thus, a Mr Makwana, Minister of State for Home was reported as saying 'that the Sadhupur carnage was clearly a case of 'motivated' killings ... the Government would leave no stone unturned to find out what the exact motive was and who the motivators were'. (IE, 2:7D) A day after she advanced the 'cousin sister's husband' theory Mrs Bakshi made one more attempt at understanding this piece of recalcitrant reality, one more attempt to locate the 'meaningless' killings in a signifying context:

> ...the incident appeared to be politically motivated. She pointed out that the killers entered the village at the time the Prime Minister was addressing a public meeting in Lucknow.
>
> (HT, 3:8G)

The very next day, her fertile brain had produced yet another theory, a more specific variant of the kind of appropriation which we have noticed earlier:

> ...the 'logical conclusion' of the circumstances involving the wanton killings was that a political force believing in violence and having a fascist and anti-democratic character was behind the murders.
>
> (IE, 4:1C)

In a few days, however, the promise of this theory had dissipated, and a police spokesman was reduced to making the limp claim: 'There is nothing to controvert the theory'. (PAT, 9:4F) On the same day, in another paper, the Home Secretary made the same claim about another theory - that the murders had been committed by Anar Singh's gang: it, too, had not been contradicted by the evidence. (IE, 9:1A) The possibilities of low comedy in this kind of negative investigation are endless - and match perfectly the kinds of comic appropriation which were taking place at other points on the political spectrum. Mr. A.B. Vajpayee asked the Thakurs and the Jatavas - the killers and their victims - to kiss and make up (HT, 9:8E), because, of course, the evil was wholly without, and there were no snakes in his Garden of Eden. Mr. Suresh Ram, son of Jagjiwan, was reported to have persuaded the naive and terrified Jatava, who had received Rs 8500 as compensation, to hand the money over to him, in return for the promise of more from the Babu Jagjiwan Ram Mass Violence Relief Fund (TOI, 6:4C) - he later denied the whole story. The President of the Virat Hindu Samaj, Raja Karan Singh, sanctioned an amount of Rs 5000 to be distributed among the untouchable victims of the Sadhupur 'carnage'. (PAT, 9:10E)

This is tedious but it is not, I suggest, irrelevant - because each of these pathetic, paltry attempts at the appropriation of our central event, each grotesque reduction of its tragic significance to narrow, familiar parameters, embodies a specific attempt also, whether explicitly or implicitly, at imposing a particular meaning on that event, a specific attempt at understanding a complex, multi-dimensional reality.

However, newspapers do not merely report the views of others with regard to the 'facts' which they render into 'news'. Nor do they confine themselves entirely to the lethally banal prose of the agency handout, that stolid bureaucratese in which everything comes out grey and featureless. They do make attempts to structure the act of attention which they would ideally like to induce in the reader. Thus, the *Indian Express* of the 2nd January reported:

> Ten dead Harijans lay wrapped in new cloth as their relatives in dirty and tattered attire waited solemnly for the helicopters to descend from the skies .....
>
> (IA)

The juxtapositions are clearly 'meant' - the dead bodies, the whirring ministerial helicopters, the new shrouds, the ragged garments of the living. Another paper, the **Patriot**, also saw the helicopters as an essential part of the context in which the deaths were to be understood. It reported an Additional Inspector General of Police instantly busying himself on the night the murders happened, not, heaven forfend, with investigations, but with preparing a helipad for the inevitable ministerial visitants. The bodies 'await inspection', but the Inspector-General of Police assures us that 'investigations of the carnage will start seriously once these rituals are over'. (PAT, 3:lC) Now, that word 'rituals' is significant, because not only does it suggest a nicely deprecatory attitude with regard to all the ministerial fuss, it is also, faithfully reported, a knowing wink in the direction of the reader, a little gesture of complicity which implicates the reader, and introduces yet another dimension into the act of attention through which, as it were, the 'carnage' is being apprehended - indeed, constituted.

The *Indian Express* correspondent, reporting from Sadhupur itself on 3 January, seemed to go to the emphatic heart of the matter when be identified caste-hatred as the critical fact about the tragic killings. However, this potentially analytical insight was squandered in the report itself, which consisted largely of explaining why the Harijans were the obvious victims for a rising wave of Thakur anger - a variant of the familiar strategy by which the victim is blamed for having brought the suffering upon himself. The clumsiness of the analytical operation is mirrored in the absurd metaphor with which he opens his report:

> The virus of caste hatred which exploded in Deoli and which left in its wake more than 24 Harijans dead is spreading fast.
>
> (IE, 4:7B)

A virus which explodes and leaves a wake? - I suggest it is not mere pedantry to baulk at this, and ask whether the metaphors, clashing along, are advancing understanding, or merely obfuscating it. The viral/disease metaphor, the (warlike ?) violence of the explosion, communicate the necessary sense of urgency, serve the function of emotional arousal - but as regards identifying the crucial social processes whereby and wherein murderous longings are generated and gratified, or offering any guidance as regards active interventions, the virus and the explosion simply cancel each other out, annihilate each other in a futile ecstasy of emotion.

The most serious and studied attempt to get at, to distil the meaning of these melancholy happenings was made, in my opinion, by Harish Khare, writing in the *Hindustan Times* of 10 January - 'Death in Sarhupur'. (There is one point I would like to make clear - now, before it is too late. If I criticise the semiological appropriations of others, it is not from a sense of superiority, a smug delusion that I am less prone than others to that variously determined particularity of perception which characterises all attempts at understanding reality. If this intellectual project has any justification at all, it is simply that one can see the motes in other people's eyes better than one can in one's own. With that caveat, therefore, I will proceed).

The immediately gratifying feature of Khare's report is the sense which he conveys of the difficulty of his enterprise. In what way can such events, really, be understood? Is it enough to note the precise name and location of the village, the names of the dead, the names of the killers? Can analysis ever be adequate, or must one, ineluctably reach out towards poetry and surrealism to articulate the grotesque truth of these happenings? Clearly, the genre within which one is working carries within it some in-built limitations - the journalist writing to meet a deadline cannot afford the brooding, meditative intensity which a novelist can bring to his task. But, even so, I find in the circling, fragmentary form which Khare employs, an awareness of the elusive nature of reality, even one as evidently 'available' as these sudden, violent deaths.

The approach is foregrounded - 'Take the Delhi-Kanpur-Calcutta road, National Highway Number 2'. Even as we pick up circumstantial detail - The dirt road that connects the village to the highway is full of potholes; the short journey is rather rough' - we are, **simultaneously**, being placed in a specific relationship, not only with the observing consciousness, but also with that reality which we are moving to encounter: 'On the way to Sarhupur **you** see families - mothers, fathers and children trekking out of the neighbouring villages. **They** are carrying their life's savings...' (italics added)

The journalist backs off, as if unwilling to intrude with such callow impatience - there is a section of background material on Anar Singh, that shadowy but violent figure whose presence hovers over these grisly events. There follows, cold, a caste-profile of the village, fractured beyond all possibilities of community, except in sentimental idealisations. The journalist, looking for his clue, probes with ironies - the unkempt villager, recounting his 'incoherent' grief to an immaculately dressed Minister. The Minister will go away to Lucknow, the unkempt villager has lost three children. Reaching for the main events, Khare briefly notes something that might well be significant - that on that fateful evening, all the men were away at a meeting to iron out some problems relating to the work they did for the glass-bangle factories of Firozabad. No simple peasants, these - but, while this detail was noted by a couple of papers, not one of them followed it up. Urban violence we can understand - the slum-lords, the union-bashing goon squads, the riots - and we can understand rural violence - the traditional, revealed violence of a degenerate feudal society under pressure. But new meanings, new forms of understanding can only emerge when, under pressure from an evolving reality, new categories, new arrangements, new 'plots' have crystallised.

It is ironic that in seeking to get to the heart of the matter, Khare has to resort to reenacting the crime, to retracing the steps of the violent intruders, albeit armed only with a tape-recorder and an observant eye - as if seeking to know in this imperative fashion were also a kind of violence. We enter one house, three children die. We enter the next one, and the woman who is cooking at the *chulha* ends up bleeding to death while the food gets charred. Another house, more deaths - and we notice as we leave, the pathetic possessions which remain. The journalist resorts, again, to indirection - to subverting with an angry irony the political scavengers who are seeking, in their own callous ways, to appropriate the tragedy. These are, it must be said, soft targets for irony - even though they are eminently deserving of irony, and worse - and Khare's resort to it suggests,among other things, the rugged intractability of the central event. Still, to identify the scavengers as context, to locate the tragedy in a necessary relation to these systematic, ritualistic inhumanities, is to endow it with yet another kind of meaning. The text is modified by its context.

We are back, ultimately, with the conditions of discourse, the communication situation itself which sets an absolute limit, as it were, on the possibilities not merely of communication but also, implicitly, retrospectively, also of perception and meaningful understanding. Every communication situation necessarily carries encoded within it certain norms, certain unspecified but specific notions of plausibility and coherence. And it would be an act of willful naivete to believe that the minority English press which has, for better, for worse, a certain class audience, is an exception. I think that Adorno's position in the following extract is overstated, and allows insufficient room for the possibility and reality of dissent, but it contains, nevertheless, an important insight into the intimate dialectic between thought and the possibilities of communication:

> Not only does the mind mould itself for the sake of its marketability, and thus reproduce the socially prevalent categories. Rather, it grows to resemble...the status quo even where it subjectively refrains from making a commodity of itself. The network of the whole ... leaves the individual consciousness less and less room for evasion, preforms it more and more thoroughly, cuts it off *a priori* as it were from the possibility of differencing itself...[6]

To become aware of these limits, however, to become aware of the pressures and the implicit silences of the socially available categories, requires a struggle at the roots of the mind, of consciousness itself, because what is at issue is the shape of reality itself, and the processes whereby amorphous reality is endowed with that formed, familiar quality, the solace of recognition.

'Carnage', said the papers - a good, strong word, adequate to carry the necessary emotional charge, the sense of accumulated brutality, etc. However, this charge was more often than not diminished by the phrase 'an incident of carnage'. Incident ? I shall take shelter behind the authority of the OED:

1. Something that occurs casually in connection with something else; an event of accessory or subordinate character.

2. An occurrence viewed as a separate circumstances.

I do not think I am being pedantic and fussy when I insist the in describing the Sadhupur killings as an 'incident', one is performing an ideological - here, precisely, a decontextualising - manoeuvre. It might be urged at this point that an 'incidental' view of reality is ingrained, inevitable in the genre of the newspaper. May be . But then it is crucial to recognise that this disconnection is not ideologically neutral. This amorphousness, the inhibited perception of pattern, itself becomes a kind of shaping, a studied, tendentious anarchy. (The formal parallel with the functioning of pluralist democracy in late-capitalist societies might be noticed here.) The refusal or inability to see the systematic linkages works to suppress the violence which is inherent and ingrained in the 'normal' situation itself. An insistence on seeing these linkages, a refusal to see the killings as an 'incident', even of carnage, but rather as part of a pattern of inhumanity, would also be an ideological manoeuvre, a deliberate attempt to press a particular reading, a specific understanding of reality

Repeatedly, in narrating rural violence, we notice that commentators resort to the form of the shattered idyll - '... the small and sleepy village ...' (IE, 4:7B) where, as the shades of dusk gather, the men assemble at the *chaupal* to discuss matters of consequence, the children huddle around the family *chulha* while the women cook the evening meal, and tell stories no doubt - then, suddenly, this cosy domesticity is violently intruded upon, violated, irretrievably shattered - irretrievable, that is until the next time. Khare is, as it happens, possessed of a powerful insight, in the form of a line from Graham Greene's **The Comedians**: 'Violent deaths are natural deaths here'. It is an insight which, assimilated, could transform the very basis on which the central event has been understood. But in order for that insight to be assimilated, the conditions of discourse themselves would have to be altered, the communication situation reconstituted. The good, conscientious, not inhumane newspaper reader is no doubt outraged by the 'carnage' but he also shares a dig at the political scavengers with the policeman - to say nothing of his perhaps inarticulate and ambivalent and contradictory commitment to the social condition of which the 'carnage' is an integral, regrettable, part. It is a delicate equilibrium - and the corresponding ideological structures must necessarily be fabricated with the same degree of delicacy. So, the idyllic village persists, in the face of traumatic violence, the privileged child of ideology, the necessary ground of that other necessary myth - the myth of the alien disrupter, the 'Naxalite". This is dangerous terrain, because here one is approaching a sort of limit of ideology. Forced beyond this point, ideology is compelled to recognise itself. In a perceptive speculation on the 'threshold of ideology', a Western critic has ventured the optimistic opinion that ideology 'cannot survive the traumatic recognition of its own repressed parentage ...'[7] But if it does, as is likely in fecund, tropical conditions, it is liable to turn nasty.

The question which we need to ask is - how much of 'reality' are we trying to understand - how far, in time and distance, and we prepared to follow the antecedent chains of circumstance which culminated in a traumatic 'newsworthy' event; what weight and consequence do we attach to the variably self-conscious attempts to grasp and form the event and its resonances, its reverberations. The answers one gives will be determined by one's ideological predispositions - and will, once made, reinforce and perhaps modify those predispositions. Because the point, finally, is that 'reality' isn't simply waiting passively 'out there' - it is, in one sense, indifferent, persisting under the influences of its inherent dynamic; in another sense, it needs to be constituted by our acts of attention, the sensitivity which we, as readers and citizens, can bring to the varied and complex and paradoxical transactions between texts and contexts. 'Reality' is transfigured, formed by our acts of understanding. So also, in important respects, are we.

NOTES

(Newspaper references are contained in the body of the text itself. The abbreviated names of newspapers expand obviously enough - TOI : *The Times of India*; HT :*Hindustan Times*; IE: *Indian Express*; PAT: *Patriot*; ST: *The Statesman*. All references are to the Delhi editions. The first digit in the reference identifies the date, the second the page number, and the final letter the column from which the quotation is taken. Thus, 3: 4F refers to the sixth column on page 4 of the newspaper issue of 3 January 1982.)

1. *The Review of Metaphysics* 24 (1971); cited by Quentin Skinner, 'Language and Social Change', in L. Michaels and C. Ricks ed. *The State of the Language*, University of California Press, 1979, p. 576.

2. 'Introduction' to A.C.H. Smith, et. al., *Paper Voices: The Popular Press and Social Change 1935-65*, London, 1975, p.18.

3. See *The Great War and Modern Memory* (1975).

4. 'Isn't the news terrible ?' a review of *More Bad News* by the Glasgow University Media Group, in *London Review of Books*, II, 13, (July 1980), p.6.

5. 'Critical Linguistics', in R. Fowler, et.al. ed., *Language and Control*, (London, 1979), p. 190.

6. T.W. Adorno, *Prisms*, (London, 1967), p.21

7. Terry Eagleton, *Criticism and Ideology*, (London, 1976), p.96.

NINE

S. Radhakrishnan

SOCIAL REALITY AND PUBLIC POLICY

The effort to understand the universe entails the unravelling of the mysteries of the physical world and of life in its myriad manifestation. Curiosity, an outgrowth of human cognitive ability led human beings to explore the earth and the skies and reflect on the human condition. Systematic exploration of the physical universe resulted in the development of natural sciences and contemplation on and observation of the human condition took the shape of philosophy and the social sciences. The social sciences aim to understand social reality by scientific methods of inquiry.

The development of the social sciences was directly related to the developments in the socio-political organization of humankind. These developments were related to the human ability to innovate in respect of eking out a livelihood on earth. Starting with the need to find food to exist and the need to procreate, human needs multiplied and human ingenuity kept pace with the desire to satisfy them. Discovering the laws of nature and applying such knowledge to meet the needs of humans resulted in the development of technology that was utilised to meet not just the imperatives of human existence and perpetuation of the species, but to meet the sophisticated needs for organized living.

Wherever human life manifested itself and numbers increased, societies came into being. The search for food and shelter brought with it the need for protection and defence against competitors. This in turn necessitated political organization and created the state as distinct from society. The social sciences emanated from the mutual interaction of state and society in the Western World. The social sciences as a group of disciplines distinct from the humanities first took shape in the Western industrial states. Their influence later permeated the developing countries along with the adoption of democratic systems of government and acceptance of the concept of popular sovereignty.

Systematization of knowledge in the area of social sciences came about largely under the impetus of the Industrial Revolution and the movements towards the realization of popular sovereignty. Contemplation on social organization held out the possibility of the development of a science of society based on scientific understanding of social reality. The French philosopher Augustus Comte was one of the earliest protagonists of this hope. It was generally believed, as the study of social organization was taken up, that it was possible to scientifically systematise knowledge in the area of the activities of the individual as a member of a group.

The functions of the state have a direct bearing on social reality, the perception of which is made by the social scientist who aims to study it scientifically and the policy maker who aims to utilise the perception of it in the discharge of the functions of the state.

The functions of state have changed and evolved over the years, by and large in keeping with a broad consensus in society in respect of them. It has veered over the year between those of a police state, a social welfare state, and a socialist/communist state. organized life brought in its wake domination and subordination of classes ands their differentiation into the rulers and the ruled. The need for maintaining law and order within organized groups and for providing defence against competing groups legitimised the role of political authority. The settlement of nomadic man to agriculture and allied activities brought in the feudal system. This in turn led to the legitimisation of kings and monarchs as political authority providing law and order and protection in return for allegiance and contribution of revenue. When the feudalist mode of production gave way to the capitalist mode the functions of the state also underwent concomitant changes. Concepts of popular sovereignty emerged and from it developed the concept of civil society, the consent of which has necessary for the exercise of political power. The Hobbesian concept of the people's sovereignty which provided the justification for absolute monarchy gave way to Lockian concept of the consent of the governed. Throughout the development of capitalism and the establishment of the modern state John Locke's theory of the contract predominated political thinking. This was so because he expounded the theory of people's rights of which the pivot was that of the right to private property. This right constituted the core of the ideology of capitalism.

In the heyday of capitalism, the dominant theory of state was that of **laissez-faire**. This reduced the legitimate functions of the state to the minimum of maintaining law and order and such other allied activities. It was argued by the protagonists of this theory that the purposes of society were best served by minimum interference by the state in its activities, thereby providing the maximum freedom of choice.

The inequities that the Industrial Revolution and the capitalist mode of production based on it perpetrated in society necessitated an ethical review of the old premises of **laissez-faire**, and the concept of the welfare state came to be adopted in its place in most states where the Industrial Revolution had stretched its arm. The state assumed responsibility for a minimum standard of individual and communal welfare and this constituted the basic theoretical premise of the social welfare state.

The right to property and the individual freedom of choice which formed the core of capitalism became issues of major attack under marxism. According to Marx, capitalism took two contrary turns. The increased adoption of state welfare in some states and the reaffirmation of **laissez faire** modified partially to meet changed circumstances in others. Based on the theories of Marx and Engels a new concept of the state centring round public ownership of the means of production and distribution was introduced in Russia. Denouncing the system of private property as incapable of providing welfare to all, the state took on the function of enforcing welfare. Such a state under Marxian theory was ultimately to whither away with the establishment of classes society.

In the light of the foregoing changes in the role and functions of the state, the need of understanding social reality for the purpose of formulating and implementing public policy is self-evident. The view of social reality would have varied vastly depending upon the functions the state has been called upon to play from time to time. The systematic collection of information relating to socio-economic conditions to inform government policy emanated in countries where popular sovereignty formed the basis of governmental authority. Britain sets the trend in this regard. The emergence of the social sciences as a distinct category of knowledge apart from the humanities can be traced to the early efforts in Britain and Europe to understand the impact of the Industrial Revolution and the capitalist mode of production on society as a whole.

Advances in the natural sciences and the consequent development in technologies affected socio-political organization significantly. The innovations resulting from the discoveries of the physical laws of the universe and their practical applications culminated in the Industrial Revolution which radically changed society. People reacted to its impact on society with conservative, liberal and radical predilections. These differing predilections characterized the different perceptions of social reality.

Those with a conservative bent of mind were against the changes brought in by industrialism and democracy and stood for the old order of tradition and authority. The liberals stood for democracy, capitalism, industrialism and individualism. the radicals accepted industrialism and technology, but not capitalism. Their concept of democracy differed from the liberal one in that they accepted it only in so far as authority had its base in the people as a whole.

Those predilections had profound significance for the efforts to understand social reality by scientific collection of data and analyses. Individual predilections have their origins in individual temperaments, and this makes for significant variations in the perception of the same social reality existing in a particular society at a particular point in time.

Apart from individual predilections based on individual psychology, currents of thought that influence the creation of knowledge also have a significant influence on the perception and understanding of social reality. The three major currents of thought that influenced the social sciences in their effort to understand social reality were positivism, humanitarianism and the philosophy of evolution. Conservative and liberal thinking related primarily to these currents and took positions on social reality largely within these frameworks. The radical predilection was concretised theoretically under the Marxian framework of analysis and became a distinct method of understanding social reality.

Predilections constitute one set of factors that condition the perception of social reality. Values are another. In the initial accommodation of humans in respect of organized living in society can be traced the genesis of the value system. Perception of reality is conditioned by values, and values in turn emanate from observed reality. Values have their linkage with predilections as well. The history of human life on earth would indicate that societal formations took place all over the world with specific value systems and norms based on the particular needs of organized living in respect of particular environments. The need to live in accommodation with fellowhumans, however, appears to have had universal validity.

As human beings in society perceived social reality, limited to begin with by predilection based on individual psychology and an imbibed value system, the knowledge acquired interacted with perception and led to the formulation of theory. The theoretical formulation thus framed became the reference frame for further inquiry. It may be said that all theoretical frameworks are conditioned in one way or the other by predilection, ideology, value and perceived facts. This has innate significance for the understanding of the possibilities and limitations of social science effort to understand social reality.

Social science inquiry being conditioned, as it is, by the particular nature of the inquirer's perception and scale of vision, can then be assessed for its ability to fathom social reality only on the basis of an understanding of the limits or more positively, the possibilities of the human beings cognitive ability to understand individual and collective life on earth.

Just as it has not been possible yet for natural science to fathom a significant part of the physical world, so has it not been possible to understand a human being as an individual and a social being in totality. While natural science seems to lend itself to deterministic laws which have universal applicability in terms of physical reality, social science is still in the process of grappling with the multitude of variable that emanate from the individual human being's cognitive ability and its interaction with the universe. Social reality, therefore, seems to elude scientific laws with any significant degree of universality.

In stating this it is important to keep in mind the fact that while in natural science inquiry the inquirer concentrates on a seemingly constant physical reality changing under definable laws that have universal applicability, in social science inquiry the effort is to understand the lives of fellow humans who are themselves perceiving so cial reality constituted by the infinitude of conditions relative to such perception. This is why social reality eludes scientific systematisation to a greater degree than physical reality.

Within the limitations indicated above, the possibilities of scientific social inquiry have been proved to be significant. The social sciences have successfully reached out not only to understand the culture-specific peculiarities of human beings and their social, economic and political organizations, but also the underlying universals that define the human species.

However, a gap exists between the social scientific effort and the perception of social reality, and this has significance for its use or utilization for public policy. Several factors are responsible for this gap. Some are inherent in the very nature of human perception as mentioned earlier. Others stem from the tools of inquiry and methods of social science research. The fact that social reality is multifaceted is self evident. The fact that it is ever-changing or seeming to be so has direct relevance to the inability of the social scientific effort to enframe it in a static mould. To distinguish the fundamental from the seemingly changing phenomena is an arduous task necessitating a multipronged incessant effort. Knowledge as it has developed in the social sciences has resulted from unidisciplinary efforts at understanding social reality. Segments of the reality are unravelled by such efforts, and a coordinated picture of several such efforts fails to do justice to empirical social reality. Rigour of methods in a single social science discipline does contribute to the development of insights into a facet of a problem, but public policy concerns itself with the whole problem and can make only limited use of it. Too much emphasis on a unidisciplinary approach in the social sciences results in the alienation of the social sciences from social reality as a whole. It does, however, increase the knowledge available to a community which is important as a component in the education that is imparted to its members. It also has, thus an indirect relevance for public policy, as the policy maker as a product of the educational system would have imbibed the social science culture to some extent. Micro-level understanding of the social reality can contribute to the development of insight in policy making provided an effort is made by policy maker to evaluate all such studies relevant to the problem in respect of which policy is to be formulated.

The origins of intellectual exploration of humankind was holistic. The objective was a largeness of comprehension combined with a keenness of perception. Rigour in developing the keenness of perception led to specialisation in particular areas of social inquiry and while awareness that all human phenomena are multidisciplinary existed, the effort to understand life and society got segmented. The need for reaffirming the multidisciplinary of human affairs is felt deeply now when problems related to human affairs appear to elude successful handling with the instrument of public policy.

For results of social scientific effort to be utilised for public policy, the prime need is its successful communication. Communication is the transfer of a thought content from one person or a group of persons to another person group of persons. This entails couching the information in language that is precise and clear and intelligible to the non-expert in the field and ensuring that it is disseminated through appropriate media. With the revolution in methods of communication the scope for such dissemination has increased to an extent unimaginable in the days when the print medium was the only one available for the purpose. The responsibility for this rests with the social science community which should explore way and means to activate the processes that help in the achievement of the goal of effective communication with the public as well as the policy maker.

Communication as a facilitating agent for the dissemination of the results of research has not till recently been taken up for study by social scientists. Communication involves the processes of conveying the results of the thought processes which involves in turn the understanding of the psychological process of thinking and communicating as related to human beings. It is generally known that only a small segment of the internal dialogue within human beings is communicated to the external world. This being so, to understand social reality with a degree of depth, the very process of human communication with its psychological mainsprings should be understood. The transmission of the thought processes with the science of language or linguistic rigour is of great significance in conveying the exact connotation of words and phrases used. The need for this was felt in the field of philosophy and in course of time in the social sciences. Linguistic philosophy, linguistic anthropology and sociolinguistics have contributed to the understanding of the culture specific attributes of ideas and language in general and have advanced the ability to understand social reality. The social sciences had neglected study of these aspects of communication and this is one of the factors that contribute to the gap in social science research and the perception of social reality.

When the fact that an individual communes with himself internally (or with God transcendentally), with other fellow beings at an interpersonal level, and with society at large at various levels such as the family, the tribe, the nation and the world is taken into consideration the importance of communication in the understanding of social reality becomes evident.

The social science effort to study social reality and communicate it to the public and the policy maker inevitably entails time that is inordinately long for the imperatives of policy making. Besides, such efforts can at best be diagnostic and analytical and can seldom be prescriptive. Its influence on public policy can be considered significant only if taken as one of the many inputs that go into public policy formulation.

While differentiating the use of social science research and social scientists in policy formulation it may be said that the 'possibilities' of social science in tackling the problems of society are generally overstated. That social science research can contribute to social engineering is a hope and claim that appears to have been belied in many Western societies, as judged on the basis of the social science effort made so far. The scientific method and unquestioned normative values have a long way to go to be able to understand and find prescriptions for human problems in society.

There is often a hiatus between the concept of the ideal based on predilection and ideology that provides the value for the framework of inquiry and the actual reality as perceived by empirical evidence. The ideal provides the ultimate objective to be met by social action and is necessary as a rationale for human endeavour to improve the condition of humankind on earth. The social science effort addresses itself to analysis and diagnosis of the existing reality. It falters in the area of prediction and prescription. This is so because the research inquiry is often sectoral and prediction and prescription have value, particularly for public policy to any significant extent, only it relates to the whole. It is also not always possible to make a rational prediction or a prescription based on a segmented inquiry as the whole constantly interacts with the segment (and vice versa) and changes the reality that has been analysed or diagnosed over time.

Social science research is not to be equated to social action. Under the early influence of humanitarianism the frameworks of research and social action were not clearly differentiated. With the influence of positivism, the need to prove the feasibility of the desirable ends influenced social science perception of social reality in a significant way. The impact of the philosophy of evolution on social scientific inquiry while not overpowering has left its indelible mark and provides the opposing trend in which intellectual effort in philosophy and social sciences has developed in respect of public policy in particular.

II

The policy maker's perception of social reality will perforce be pragmatic as compared to that of the social scientist. It would relate to the consensus on functions of the state that exists in the society in which he or she operates and to the priorities of the particular government of which he or she is a part. It would vary considerably in relation to whether he operates in a pluralistic democratic system, a socialist or a communist system.

The development of the social sciences on conservative, liberal and radical predilection was reflected in the evolution of governmental policies. The ideas generated by intellectuals in a society create the issues that engage politicians and administrators. The issue that agitate politicians also get examined by intellectuals. Political ideas and theories provide the intellectual atmosphere for the governors and the governed. But public policy is circumscribed by the concept of the 'possible'. While intellectuals may define for the policy maker what is possible based on their own criteria the policy maker tests this against the touchstone of political and administrative feasibility.

Whatever the limitations of public policy in absorbing or utilising social science research, its scope for implementing social, economic and political ideas is very significant. The history of the 20th century provides ample evidence for this. The development and implementation of the concept of the welfare state within the Western liberal democracies and establishment of the socialist and communist states are cases in point. Public policy as an instrument for economic and socio-political action has come to stay notwithstanding rethinking on some dimensions of it in recent times.

The policy maker in government does require adequate perception of the social reality within which he or she functions. Social science research which purports to study social reality could, therefore, be a significant inputs into public formulation and implementation. However, the policy makers perception of the reality would comprise the insights which the social science research results may have provided, insights into the politically important as well as their feasibility. In this order of importance the subjective factors of the government's particular priorities would predominate. The objective reality would assume secondary importance. However, they would require data and analyses and some theory to operationalise policy. Without a framework of theory there would be no sense of direction in the formulation of policy. It would also be difficult to evaluate impact of policy. Policies based on insights into social reality provided by social science research effort, albeit based on limited understanding of the multifaceted reality, have an advantage in implementation over those totally bereft of such insights.

Public policy at a given point in time would reflect the dominant ideology of the government in power. In a pluralistic democratic society with groups competing for political representation of special interests, the government in power is concerned with the dilemma of implementation of election promises and continuing political support. While in theory a broad concept of the 'public good' is the guideline for democratic governments returned to power by the majority, in practice, balancing of interests for continuance in power becomes the overriding concern.

In socialist/communist systems there is generally a broad consensus on the framework of public policy. Within this accepted framework the social science research effort attempts to focus on the strategies and priorities in respect of realization of the laid down goals. The attempt to unravel the objective reality as it presents itself is circumscribed by the framework and method of inquiry that are integral to the whole system. The social reality thus unravelled affirms the accepted framework and leads in the long run to considered alterations and adjustments within it. The human desire for fundamental reflection on life and society, however, does question the accepted framework of public policy and take the shape of dissent from the establishment.

How valid is the objective of the 'public good' for public policy in reality? If all of social scientific effort at understanding social reality was directed towards the ultimate end of an objectively or otherwise determined public good for a particular society and all governmental policy was directed towards meeting this end, social science and public policy would be more in step than out of step with each other and the controversy over the utilisation of the research effort would not arise. It is precisely because there never is any one conclusive social scientific view in respect of any policy issue and no one optimum policy in respect of it that the effort towards a proper fit between public policy and social reality is so arduous.

To understand social phenomena with any degree of generalizability data has to be collected and analysed within a framework of theory. In pluralist societies with the democratic system of government this make the contribution of social science to the development of policy relative to different frameworks. It is generally believed that objective, rational thought should be the basis for the development of policy. In actuality in a pluralistic system, public policy at any given point in time may reflect, to the extent, any one of many competing frameworks. Differing objectives and constraints of pressures stand in the way of the development of public policy with a permanent framework. Policy ultimately is the result of contrary interests, ideals and goals compromised on the basis of political acceptability.

It follows, therefore, that even if the social sciences did succeed in narrowing the gap in the perception of social reality and were able to give the benefit of a broader vision of it for use for policy, public policy would at no point be able to fully utilise it. Ideas presented to the policy maker are invariably purged of their unacceptable content to be made politically and administratively acceptable within the relevant framework of policy. Thus, social scientific effort and public policy function within the constraints of their respective 'frameworks'.

The two, however, interact and the extent of the impact of one on the other would depend upon the nature of the social science inquiry. Fundamental research in the social sciences, while it takes cognizance of policy, past and present, need not necessarily be conditioned by public policy. It can create new knowledge and provide new insights and, though influenced by policy can stand independent of it. Research that purports to unravel the objective reality in the interest of providing the advise for meeting the objective of the public good has the potential to influence public policy in a general sense. It would find a place in the teaching system and some extent in the broad policy statements of government. Such research, while it may be noted by the affirm the accepted official 'framework' for policy. It may also be that research, while it may be noted by the policy maker may not be utilised unless the findings affirm the accepted official 'framework' for policy. It may also be that research findings that confirm personal beliefs and opinions have a greater scope for acceptance than those that contradict them. The maximum interaction would be in the case of policy-oriented research which engages itself in the immediate requirements of the governments in power vested with the responsibility of formulating and implementing policy.

While the two distinct perceptions of the same social reality by social scientists and policy makers may differ significantly on the basis of methods and purpose, social reality in the ultimate analysis is a synthesis of the manifold perceptions of all its facets. Its utilisation for policy varies from state to state. Developed societies use it for purposes that differ from the use made of it by developing societies. Also, unlike in the developing societies where applications of social science have many times belied expectations, in developing societies there is greater reliance on its possibilities and hope in respect of its function and utility.

Policy maker and social scientists often forget the fact that policy makers rest on a social science inundated stock of knowledge. When decisions are taken on policy, the premises are taken for granted and the extent to which the social sciences have contributed to the premises are not often recognized. The impact of fundamental research is also more often than not of universal validity, contributing to theory which is vital for the development of policy.

III

A widely accepted premise is that public policy in the ultimate analysis emanates from a framework of thought common to the social scientist and the policy maker based on the reflections on life and society contributed by the world's philosophers and humanists. The concept of 'justice' individual and social may be considered the core concept on which paradigms of social scientific thought coverage and differ.

The quest for justice appears to have begun with the beginning of human thinking and organization. The consensus on norms and values that resulted from organized life in society led to the development of concepts of individual and social justice. Speculations on it over the years emerged in two broad trends - The belief that justice was an absolute concept such as truth and that it was relative and specific to societies with differing concepts of norms and values. These trends have had a profound influence on the development of ideas on social, economic and political organization.

The philosophic divide in the analysis of social reality is relevant for the understanding of its impact on public policy. The Western democratic-liberal approach and the socialist-communist approach differ significantly in respect of what is perceived as the reality. Social scientific effort based on these differing approaches are not geographically compartmentalised activities, but are interactional in a universal sense. The results of social scientific thought feed in both strands of thinking.

Social scientific effort is carried on largely within its own frameworks based on values and without a norm to judge values. Justice as a concept is deemed desirable in general. Not much thought has gone into inquiring why. There never was a consensus on exactly what is connoted by the concept. The concepts of individual and social justice are, however, integrally related to prevailing ideas at any point in time on legitimacy of power equations, differentiation of functions and division of labour, etc. It is also related integrally to the philosophic concept of the equality of all humankind.

Would justice then require that social action should ensure the survival of the human species rather than that of the fittest among them? The concept of evolution if applied to human beings and society would amount to equating human life and destiny on earth to that of the rest of the animal world hitherto manifest. Human beings using their cognitive abilities appear from hindsight to have been motivated by the urge for the survival of their species. Humankind's effort towards organized living appears to have been one of the early steps in this direction. The search for norms of universal validity appear to be promoted by the urge to find ways and means to avoid extinction like many earlier manifestations of life on earth. In fact, humankind's cognitive ability appears in the main to have been geared to this major preoccupation in its age-long search for the meaning of life and death. In this search it would appear that humankind has been divided largely into those not conscious of need for active human endeavour for the survival of the species an those deeply conscious of it. The conservative strain of thought that underlies public policy would seem consciously or unconsciously to justly the survival of the fittest as a law of nature. The liberal trend in public policy (which includes the radical as well in this regard) would seem to believe that the destiny of humankind can be influenced by human effort and would appear to carry on with the faith that is possible by right policies to ensure the survival of the human species.

This observation assumes great relevance in the present-day world poised on the precipice of the abyss of total destruction. The acceptance of the survival of the species as a unified goal for humankind is the need of the times. As normative values such as social, economic and political justice break down with change and new values based on consensus take long to emerge, and would emerge only if there is a consensus for organized living, the imperative need to link social science inquiry for the understanding of social reality with the destiny of humankind cannot be over-emphasized. The existential crisis of humankind would require the wisdom that comes from the combination of social reality with the destiny of humankind cannot be over-emphasized. The existential crisis of humankind would require the wisdom that comes from the combination of social scientific and humanistic disaster. Survival of humankind could be the fundamental value within the framework of which social scientific inquiry and public policy could interact and work together providing the purpose and justification for values such as justice and equality for humankind.

REFERENCES

Encyclopedia of the Social Sciences.

Howard E. Freeman, and Clarence C. Sherwood, *Social Research and Social Policy*, Prentice Hall, New Jersey, 1970.

Kwasi, Wiredu, A Philosophical Perspective on the concept of Communication, *Inter-*

national Social Science Journal, Vol.XXXII, No.2, 1980

Laurence, D. Stifel, Ralph K. Davidson, and James S. Coleman, (eds.), *Social Sciences and Public Policy in the Developing World*, Lexington Books, D.C. Heath and Company, 1982.

Majid, Tehranian, The Curse of Modernity: The Dialectics of Modernization and Communication, *International Social Science Journal*, Vol. XXXII, No.2, 1980.

Martin, Rein, *Social Science and Public Policy*, Penguin Books, Ltd., Middlesax, 1976.

Martin, Rein, Methodology for the Study of the Interplay between Social Science and Social Policy. *International Social Science Journal*, Vol. XXXII. No.2, 1980.

Ralph, Adam, Language and Information Retrieval in the Social Sciences, Aslib Proceedings, 34 (9), September, 1981. pp.394-404.

Ralph, H. Beals, *Politics of Social Research*, Aldine Publishing Company, Chicago, 1969.

The New Encyclopedia Britannica, Vol.16, 1974.

INDEX